GAMERS

Mel Croucher

GAMERS

Ghosts in the Machine

Mel Croucher

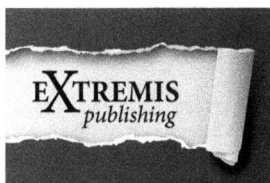

EXTREMIS
publishing

Gamers: Ghosts in the Machine by Mel Croucher
First edition published in Great Britain in 2025 by Extremis Publishing Ltd., Suite 218, Castle House, 1 Baker Street, Stirling, FK8 1AL, United Kingdom.
www.extremispublishing.com

Extremis Publishing is a Private Limited Company registered in Scotland (SC509983) whose Registered Office is Suite 218, Castle House, 1 Baker Street, Stirling, FK8 1AL, United Kingdom.

A CIP catalogue record for this book is available from the British Library.

ISBN: 978-1-0682314-4-5

Typeset in Merriweather.

Printed and bound in Great Britain by IngramSpark, Chapter House, Pitfield, Kiln Farm, Milton Keynes, MK11 3LW, United Kingdom.

CONTENTS

GAMERS

GHOSTS IN THE MACHINE

ABOUT THE AUTHOR

Mel Croucher is the acknowledged founder of the British computer games industry. Originally an architect, he moved into gaming "as a deep fake to force my music on the public."

Three-time winner of the Game Of The Year Award, he pioneered radio broadcasts of computer software, geocache gaming, in-game voice artists, interactive soap opera, real-world adventure quests, adware product placement, the first computer-generated movie, the first AI virtual companion and the first million-user viral marketing campaign.

He is the author of text books, technical manuals, fiction and non-fiction, and more than a thousand of his columns, investigations and cartoon strips have appeared in print over six decades.

GHOSTS IN THE MACHINE
A BRIEF INTRODUCTION

T he ancients believed that everything in heaven above and here down below is made from the four basic elements of earth, air, fire and water. When it comes to gaming, the ancients got it right, because there are only four elements in any game ever conceived. And those four elements are dice, chess, ping-pong and snake-oil. All video games are the regurgitated ingredients of the random throw of the dice, the tactical strategies of chess, the hand-eye coordination of ping-pong and the trickery of snake-oil. And the most important of the four elements is, of course, the snake-oil, the bunkum, the flim-flam, the razzmatazz, the smoke and mirrors of the games machine, the platform, the packaging, the mechanism and the hype, all of which are designed to part us gamers from our money.

And all of this can be traced back to the creative genius of twenty ghosts in the machine, because without these spectres at the feast the biggest entertainment industry the world has ever known would not exist and billions of gamers would be denied their chosen pleasures. The fact that these women and men are dead means they are ghosts, but they are not forgotten. This book tells their remarkable stories for the very first time in their own words and from the gamer perspective.

But the ancients did not only believe in earth, air, fire and water, they also believed in ghosts and in ghostly communication with the dead, and when it comes to gaming who knows if they were right.

In the Golden Age of gaming, programs were stored on magnetic tape and floppy discs, mostly in a primitive layer of iron oxide. Then when solid-state drives took over, the main chemical element changed to game-memories embedded in silicon.

If a ghost is simply the recording or memory of someone who once lived, then perhaps the dead can leave their own recordings behind in their wake, as electrical impulses in the iron and silicon of stone, glass, bricks and mortar. This theory has never been proved and neither has it been disproved, but it follows that ghosts can also be recorded in the components of the machines they once used while they were alive.

In this book, these stories of the ghosts in the machine embrace genius, love, loss, addiction, murder, scandal, suicide and a whole heap of fun. But never fear, it's all in the game.

1. 1804, Joseph captures the code
2. 1842, Ada programs the machine
3. 1857, Édouard records the sound
4. 1888, Charles animates the screen
5. 1934, Paul designs the internet
6. 1942, Hedy invents wi-fi
7. 1946, Grace writes machine code
8. 1950, Josef designs the machine
9. 1958, Willy adds gameplay
10. 1963, Lou donates the cassette
11. 1964, Mabel writes the strategy game
12. 1966, Ralph creates the console
13. 1976, Jerry adds the cartridge
14. 1980, Alice perfects the coin-op
15. 1980, Gunpei launches the handheld
16. 1981, Mike goes mainstream
17. 1982, Angelo opens the store
18. 1983, Danielle invites multiplayers
19. 1984, Doris is crowned champ
20. 2023, Twisten ghosts the machine

The First Ghost

Joseph Marie Jacquard, 1752-1834

Binary code, 1804

A h, so there you are! Away out there in the future, more than two centuries after I became the first man in the world to convert data into an art form. And may I ask you this, what advances have you achieved over all these intervening years? Will you please tell me. Perhaps you believe there have been many such achievements, but in all honesty I believe there have not. In which case allow me to answer my own question. I believe that you have not achieved very much at all. Your machines still replace humans, your air still stinks, your wars still rage, your rich still grow more rich, your poor still grow more poor.

I have been watching you carefully since I died, and it seems to me that in truth nothing much has changed since I became a ghost in my own machine. Nothing much except for one important thing, and that one important thing is your capacity for gaming. In your time you call it video-gaming, but I can assure you that everything was already in place in my day. It is not the gaming itself that has changed, but the scale of gaming that dominates your world. And this massive scale is simply the result of gaming technology. Technology that began with me.

People have always played games of course, as have so many other joyful creatures of this world, like monkeys, dolphins, butterflies, kittens and ghosts. The difference for our human species and other sentients lies in the mechanisms by which we play. The interface between our brains, our bodies and the gameplay itself. This is the only real difference to the past, present and future of gaming, because the basic concepts of gameplay always remain the same.

A few years before I achieved fame and was rewarded by the Emperor Napoleon himself for my inventions, I was happy to count amongst my friends a man called Jacques Lacombe, and it was he who wrote an encyclopedia of gaming. It contained some truly excellent diagrams and illustrations which included a great many scientific and mathematical amusements, and I learned very much from his pages. Jacques believed that the popularity of gaming in my society all began at the royal court of that old fraud Louis XIV, and then it erupted like a benign plague out of the court and spread far and wide into the cities and villages across the land, until people of all ages and classes spaffed their free time in the pursuit of gaming.

Then as now, this gaming plague was spread by technology, and in my time that technology was represented by the printing press. For a while in my younger days, I, Joseph Marie Jacquard, was a maker of printer's type. And along with all the printed lottery tickets and playing cards that I typeset, I helped facilitate the ability to print a great many table-top games. It is no idle boast to declare that France became the world leader in gaming during my long life, so I do not boast it idly.

I remember at first that mother church didn't much like this surge in gaming, and the clergy preached that gaming encouraged immorality, gambling and the sinful mingling of the sexes. But then the Jesuits saw the value of gaming as a way to indoctrinate little French girls and little French boys through fantasy images and concepts of teamwork and loyalty. By the time the Revolution came, it was the game-producers who were also making a killing.

In my day, almost all of the commercial games were variations of the classic *Jeu de l'Oie*, the Game of the Goose, which is what the English call *Snakes and Ladders*. Our printed game-boards usually featured a spiral to represent the game of life in one form or another. Players adopted an individual token or marker, and their progress was dictated by the throw of a dice as they raced to the winning spot. Gameplay was controlled by whatever the landing spots dictated, with good fortune offering extra moves and short cuts, and bad fortune punished by diversions, missed turns, fines, restarts and getting thrown out of the game altogether. I see that you still play table-top versions today, with names like *Monopoly* and *Dungeons and Dragons*, and I see too that these have spawned countless online variations to be played on your screens instead of your tables.

One of the board games I remember as a youth was called *The Game of Good Children*, which had already been played for a century or more before my time. I understood the adult themes well, which were based on greed and deceit, and where players took part in a role-playing game of distinctly suspect characters, including a cuckold, a whore and a corpse. The object of the game was to amass all the token coins in a token purse and bankrupt the other players.

And some of our role-playing games were also based on celebrities and influencers of the day. There was *The Game of Theatre*, with each printed square representing a well-known actor or a famous character, which we tried to enact if we landed on their square. And there was the infamous *Le Petit Jeu d'Amour* where players were teamed up with a member of the opposite sex and the dice determined whether they were to inflict pleasures or punishments on one another. That one got rather steamy, and I remember typesetting the rules for it myself which included the boast, "never before has there

3

been a game providing so much joy and pleasure to youth."
That was after I learned to read, of course.

My gaming childhood took place in the grand city of
Lyon by the banks of the Saône, where I spent what free time
I had with a pattern-game called *Tangram*. I had no formal
school education. To be truthful, I was illiterate until the age
of thirteen, so this game was perfect for a boy like me.
Tangram was based on geometric patterns, and was
deceptively simple. It presented me with seven differently
coloured shapes, each numbered. One square, one
parallelogram, one medium triangle, two smaller triangles
and two larger triangles. The starting layout formed a perfect
square, but the shapes could be arranged into an infinite
series of patterns. *Tangram* was introduced to our weaving
district of Lyon by Chinese silk merchants, and my family
were all master-weavers of that fashionable fabric, so I
became an early adopter of this imported game. Of the nine
children my mother bore, only my big sister and myself
survived to adulthood, and my poor mother herself died
when I was ten.

It was Jean-Marie, my sister's new husband, who not
only taught me to read but introduced me to a novel world of
ideas and skills. My father wanted me to take over his
weaving loom, but I confess that I was simply not man
enough. So Jean-Marie took me on at his printing works,
where I learned to assemble moveable type and illustration-
blocks using pattern codes that I devised myself. But I did not
earn very much money for my troubles, that is to say I
seemed to spend more than I earned. I freely admit that I
managed to get myself into rather a lot of debt, mostly
through my unique style of gaming which some would
describe as rather boring and very mathematical.

In my society it was not unusual to believe that
marriage could solve the sort of unfortunate financial
situation in which I found myself, so aged twenty-six I went
and found myself a nice middle-class widow named
Claudine, who not only had her own teeth and owned her

4

own property but also came with a most attractive dowry. Which I spent rather too quickly.

Claudine also owned a very fine *carrilons à musique*, a clockwork music box which could play any number of tunes, determined by a selection of revolving cylinders plugged in to the mechanism. The cylinder was studded with a great many tiny pins, and as it turned on its axis each pin would trigger an individual metal reed arranged in a linear scale of notes, along with miniature tuned bells, cymbals and percussive effects. An entire fairy orchestra was conjured in that box, and I was truly fascinated by the mechanism. It was a great pity that I had to sell it, but as I have already said, needs must.

I never forgot my love of the *Tangram* game, and I never lost my skills in printed pattern-coding. Neither did I deny my family heritage in the arts and crafts of silk weaving.

I waited out the so-called Reign Of Terror, when one mob went chopping the heads off another mob, and then the Revolt of Lyon, when the other mob chopped the heads off the first mob, and I made sure that I kept my own head securely attached to my neck. The following year, when utter chaos had become normal chaos, I raised my gaze again and declared myself to be an inventor. But I admit that I was not an immediate success. On the other hand, neither was I an immediate failure.

In Lyon, all of the real money was still to be made in patterned silk weaving, and it was my brother-in-law who advised me with the wise words, "the only certain way to make money from digging the soil is to corner the market in shovels." When it came to the silk industry after our French Revolution, this inspired me to get into the weaving loom business.

As the eighteenth fell into the nineteenth century, there were a number of makers of fine looms in Lyon, and they all had one thing in common, they required highly skilled weavers to control the intricate patterns of coloured threads by hand. I made my first attempt at designing a better loom in 1800, which used a rocking foot treadle to control the shuttle. None of the silk weavers I approached seemed at all interested, mostly because my loom did not operate very well, but I managed to keep my head above water by adapting my designs to weave fishing nets, and by 1803 my new business was up and running well enough for me to haul myself out of debt.

This gave me the breathing space to do some proper research and analysis. So I went back to basics, to see if I could apply the skills I had learned in patterns and gaming to the business of building a better weaving machine.

Another saying of my brother-in-law was, "if you cannot be original then you must plagiarise", and I invested the next year of my life doing exactly that.

I was not the only inventor who was fascinated by gaming patterns and the mechanisms of the music box. In my family's silk weaving district there lived a man named Basile Bouchon. While my grandfather was still alive Bouchon devised a method of controlling a loom via a roll of perforated paper tape. Silk weaving is an extremely skilled and labour-intensive process, of course, with the operator of a draw-loom forced to spend a great deal of time setting up every individual thread of the design by pulling a cord to lift each warp strand before it becomes integrated into the pattern. This can require thousands of manual operations, and after each such operation the weaving shuttle must be drawn from one edge of the fabric to the other. Intricate patterns are set out on large sheets of squared paper, and the operator must follow these patterns and translate them into a complicated matrix by the required arrangement of cord-pulls.

What Bouchon did was to apply the principal of the raised pins of a music-box cylinder to create an automated weaving machine. His idea was to pass each thread through the eye of a horizontal needle which could pivot up or down depending if there was a matching hole in the paper roll, and so forming the required pattern. But his system was so unreliable that users soon reverted to their traditional ways.

He tried to improve things by tasking his assistant Jean-Baptiste Falcon to increase the number of thread-holes and arrange them in several rows, and it was Jean-Baptiste who came up with the brilliant idea of punching the holes into rectangular cards that were joined together by hinges to form an endless loop. In fact it was such a brilliant idea that I was sure to claim it as my own.

What was not so brilliant was that this automated weaving machine needed an extra operator to control the punch cards, and that made it most uneconomical. Also, the endless pattern-loop was held as a perforated four-sided tube, so the designs were limited and not at all inspired. Jean-Baptiste only managed to sell forty of his mechanical looms before the Revolution. Poor man.

And then, also before the Revolution, there was a certain Monsieur Jacques de Vaucanson, a puffed-up toss pot of an inventor of automated mechanical toys, who was appointed inspector of Lyon's silk factories, and he proceeded to rationalise the failed mechanical loom designs.

Before his entry into our world of weaving, De Vaucanson's claim to fame was the construction of a mechanical duck which could quack, flap its wings, peck, eat, digest and shit, but it was his improved loom that interested me. He elevated the pattern cylinder so that it revolved above the loom, and eliminated the need for levers, weights and pulleys to select which silk threads would be raised and which would stay in place. He also introduced a ratchet mechanism to advance the punched matrix paper by one row each time the shuttle was thrown from one side to the other. Luckily for me his health, his career and his shitting duck were destroyed by the Revolution. On the other hand, Napoleon Bonaparte was a rather significant beneficiary, and as a result so was I.

Bonaparte decided to fight the English for domination of the lucrative silk weaving industry, and in 1802 huge orders for high-quality fabric began to pour into lucky Lyon. And that is when I seized my chance, and I scrapped my own loom designs in favour of stealing those of others.

It was obvious to me that the paper strips used by Bouchon and de Vaucanson had to be the weakest link in any industrial machine. Jean-Baptiste had been right, a looped chain of strong rectangular pasteboard cards was the perfect way to transmit the patterns automatically. And once I had perfected their design, my pathway to success was assured, and I made steady progress in rationalising and improving my automatic looms which they controlled. My preprogrammed cards were stacked in an almost limitless concertina arrangement to transmit the binary data of holes and spaces, and they were usable on an industrial scale for the very first time.

Emperor Napoleon wed his new Empress Josephine not long after her previous husband had been safely guillotined, and it took them less than a year of energetic copulation until they could copulate no more. As soon as they had exhausted their mutual pleasuring they both visited me in Lyon on the twelfth day of April 1805. Three days later, the Emperor granted the patent to my loom and awarded me a pension for life of three thousand francs. *Voila!* And not only that, I managed to negotiate a royalty of fifty francs for every one of my looms bought, and by the time Napoleon met his Waterloo in 1812 I am extremely proud to tell you that over 11,000 Jacquard machines had been sold. Both my fortune and my reputation were very much assured.

When I first launched my improved loom, the silk industry was easily the most important source of income for my city of Lyon, with over 30,000 citizens making some sort of a living from it. So it should not have been a surprise to me that most of them hated my innovation. Many were physically hostile, believing that my automated punch cards would make their skills obsolete, and what began as rumblings and protests soon turned into full scale riots. The malcontents were reinforced by other workers, and then things got completely out of control. They destroyed my workshop and nearly all my looms were smashed. When they burned my effigy in the main square I was forced to flee for my life disguised as a farmer to escape them. That's when the government called in the National Guard.

The Guard had enlisted a force of enthusiastic bourgeoise citizens who loathed the so-called working class, and they took every opportunity to shoot anything that moved and to burn everything that didn't. By the time they had done, most of the silk workshops in my city were destroyed and hundreds lay dead. But time passes and they are now all long gone, and history has been kind to me. I am the ghost in the Jacquard loom, which is still in production even in your time, all the way from Norway to Japan, and very much as I originally designed it. My massive stone statue looms over the centre of what is now the UNESCO World Heritage site of Lyon city centre. I am immortalised, and in my humble opinion, rightly so.

A few years after I died, my supporters commissioned a much more appropriate memorial than that cold statue. It was my portrait, but it was no ordinary portrait crafted by human hand, it was created entirely by the artificial intelligence of my own machine and employed 24,000 punched cards to weave my image in glorious colour, each card boasting over a thousand hole positions. Less than twenty copies have survived into your time, one of which had pride of place in the home of Mister Charles Babbage, the man who conceived the world's first general purpose computer and who adopted my punch card system for controlling his mechanisms. But that, as they say, is another story, as you are about to discover.

Au revoir. Merci beaucoup et bonne chance.

A LA MÉMOIRE DE J. M. JACQUARD.

Joseph Marie Jacquard memorial portrait.
Woven in silk using a Jacquard loom, by Michel–Marie Carquillat
of Didier, Petit et Cie, Lyon, 1839. Public domain.

Jacquard loom and punch-card data.
Smithsonian Institute catalog T11685.000,
Creative Commons Zero (CC0) license,
with kind permission for usage, gifted by Mr Arthur Wullschleger.

The Second Ghost

Augusta Ada Byron, Countess of Lovelace, 1815-1852

The computer programme, 1843

I t gives me great pleasure to welcome all of you gamers and gamblers to my story. My given name is Augusta but most know me as Ada, and I was what your male historians are wont to label a naughty girl. A very naughty girl. A little minx. They label me this because all brilliant women tend to unsettle male historians and cause discomfort among the patrimony. That and the fact I was 'highly intelligent, manipulative, aggressive, a drug addict, a gambler and an adulteress', as the British Broadcasting Corporation would have you believe. They have omitted the fact that I was also relishing an affair with my significantly older tutor when I first made the acquaintance of the great innovator Charles Babbage.

I was attending a house party having left my sixteenth year behind when I met him, the inventor of a computational mechanism, and the singular thing I immediately noticed was a magnificent machine-made portrait that decorated the wall of his dining room. Babbage explained to me that the likeness was of his hero Joseph Marie Jacquard who had invented punch-card data storage, and I explained to Babbage that his hero had failed to spot the flaw in the storage system such as to make it less than efficacious.

Babbage had a firm mouth and firm thighs, his hair was reddish, as was his face, and I deduced the latter was because his collar was too tight as were his crowded trousers. The timing of my attendance at his social gathering was fortuitous, because his engineer Joseph Clement had just ceased progress on all development of the invention that my host called his Difference Engine. This was not because Mister Clement could not fulfil his brief, indeed his craftsmanship was excellent; it was because he had not been paid.

My host's machine was a fine example of precision engineering but it was incomplete and limited in its function, being nothing more nor less than an advanced mechanical calculator of polynomial functions, more intuitive than an abacus, less intuitive than the brain of my dog.

I concluded that what the great man needed was not the services of another precision engineer, but the services of a precision intellect, namely my own. As I explained to him at the time, "This brain of mine is something more than merely mortal, as time will show."

I liked Babbage, and Babbage liked me, albeit most men liked me, if not for my beauty and my wit, then for my social standing and my fortune. My father was the notorious Lord Byron and my mother was the mathematician Lady Anne Millbanke, and my social circle was inclusive of the pioneers of electricity Andrew Crosse, Charles Wheatstone and Michael Faraday. I was also most familiar with the inventor of the stereoscopic viewing machine David Brewster, as well as an ambitious young writer with a roving eye and moist lips named Charles Dickens.

Babbage exhibited a very singular mind, which is why I became involved with him. What I did not become involved with was his fascination with the supernatural and his quest to prove the existence of demonic and ghostly beings, which is most ironic seeing as I am now a ghost myself, although not a demon. If you wish to examine his actual brain and not his mechanical one, then you will currently find one half of it at the Royal College of Surgeons and the other in the London Science Museum. My own brain is not on display, however, even though it is far more fascinating.

I exhibited my proclivities early, when I decided that I earnestly wished to fly, writing an explanation to my mother who was in the habit of referring to me as neither Augusta nor Ada, but as It.

"My dear mother, I have got a scheme to make a thing in the form of a horse with a steam engine in the inside so contrived as to move an immense pair of wings fixed on the outside of the horse, in such a manner as to carry it up into the air while a person sits on its back. I am going to begin my paper wings tomorrow and I feel almost convinced that with a year or so of experience and practice I shall be able to bring the art of flying to very great perfection."

I soon realised that paper was a useless material for heavier-than-air flying and I tested many alternative materials, including thin flexible sheets of tin. But I concluded that waterproofed canvas would be the most practicable. As for the shape of my wings, I dissected several differing species of birds to calculate the optimum proportions between the wings, the body and the weight. I also designed a control panel which contained a scrolling map and a compass, along with a steering mechanism much like that used by ancient charioteers. It is all noted, illustrated and annotated in my excellent little book *Flyology*. Did I mention that I was twelve years old at the time? Did I also mention that I had been paralysed by the measles and confined to my bed for a whole year?

I did not mind this inconvenience at all, because it gave me the opportunity for undistracted reading, learning, and the designing of new machines. However, flying machines and steam engines are mere sciences, whereas gaming and gambling is an art.

Two years after I first met Charles Babbage and played with his cogs, I allowed one of my men-friends to marry me. This was William King, Earl of Lovelace, so I was now a countess, which made me highly creditworthy and able to properly indulge my growing passion for gaming. Unfortunately I was forced to pawn the Lovelace family diamonds to cover my debts, and I admit that I lost several thousand pounds on the Epsom Derby, but I will always insist the reason for that was because I simply misread my notes and bet on the wrong horse.

I devised my own system for predicting the outcomes of horse races by calculating a matrix of the distance, the weather, the terrain and the number of runners and riders. I also factored the interval between a horse's last urination and the start of the race. My greatest problem was that the gentlemen who took my bets were not entirely honest with me, and I was always such a trusting soul when it came to matters of the turf.

It is a fact that dear Babbage never once betrayed my trust, and our *Prediction Book* for horse racing passed between us weekly. The formulae and operations contained within its pages are what a future generation would learn to call the algorithms of a computer program, but back then the computer languished incomplete in Babbage's workshop.

After I interrupted my work with him to give birth to three children in quick succession, my world changed when my mentor and friend devised his next-generation machine. He called it the Analytical Engine, and as with his understanding of Jacquard's punch-card data system, he completely failed to grasp the enormity and potential of what he proposed. I told him that mathematical science is the language of unseen relationships between things, but to use and apply that language, we must be fully able to appreciate, to feel, and to seize the unseen and the unconscious.

The Analytical Engine was designed as a device that would have filled my entire bathroom, but unlike my bathroom it was both intellectually and physically beautiful. The main components consisted of a mathematical mill, a memory store, a reading device and a printer. Basic flow control of the data was handled by three groups of Jacquard punch cards. These were number cards, variable cards and operational cards, and I immediately saw the potential for my own gaming and betting systems. Babbage's device could handle over one thousand numbers of up to fifty digits each, and it could also handle conditional branching and loops. If it had ever been completed I would have won a fortune on the horses. But of course it was never completed.

It was applauded though, and championed by a young mathematician named Luigi Menabrea, a dapper fellow with a ticklish moustache, especially when juxtaposed to my more sensitive areas. Many years after I became a ghost in Babbage's machine, the diminutive Luigi became prime minister of Italy, but that is of no consequence here. What is of consequence is the account of the machine that he published for the *Bibliothèque universelle de Genève* in 1842. It was in French, and it was rather uninspired. But of course I was fluent in French and extremely inspired, so it was nothing short of my duty to translate his words into English and to add my own, at length. In fact my published Notes were three times the length of Luigi's original work.

It is these Notes which have gone down in history as not only the first exposition of computer gaming, but also as the first computer programmes ever written. And rightly so, because as I have already shared with you, from a very early age I was a precocious genius, and by the time my notes were published in 1843 I was at the peak of my powers.

I will not bore you with any lengthy extracts from my Notes. They are freely available and the curious among you can read them by consulting your search engines and artificial intelligence services. But when you do, kindly remember that it was my human intelligence that precipitated all of what you use now. I believe that I can summarise the essence of my innovation in less than one page of distilled quotations. So I will do exactly that for you as follows. Please pay attention.

"We may say most aptly that the Analytical Engine weaves algebraical patterns just as the Jacquard-loom weaves flowers and leaves."

"It is the first proposal or attempt ever made to construct a calculating machine founded on the principle of successive orders of differences, which it can conduct in the absence of human intelligence during the performance of its calculations."

"The Analytical Engine does not occupy common ground with mere calculating machines. It holds a position wholly of its own in combining together general symbols, in successions of unlimited variety and extent."

"A new, a vast, and a powerful language is developed for future use. Thus not only the mental and the material, but theory and practice are brought into more intimate and effective connexion with each other."

"Nothing like the Analytical Engine has been hitherto proposed, or even thought of as a practical possibility, than the idea of a thinking or reasoning machine."

"It might act upon other things besides numbers. It might compose elaborate and scientific pieces of music of any degree of complexity or extent. For instance, the fundamental relations of pitched sounds in the science of harmony and musical composition are susceptible to mathematical expression and adaptations. Codes can be created for the device to handle letters and symbols along with numbers."

"The science of its operations is a science of itself, and has its own abstract truth and value. Imagination is the discovering faculty, and is that which penetrates into the unseen worlds around us."

"If it cannot give us poetry, it can give us poetical science, our best and wisest refuge from all troubles."

There now, dear reader of a future age, my conceptual

revolution in less than one page, as promised. Music, gaming and the arts, translated into digital form and manipulated by machines for your enlightenment and pleasure.

As for me, I died at just 36 years old. The drink, the sex and the opiates caught up with me. That and the uterine cancer. My friend Charles Dickens was one of the last visitors to my bedside. His intention was to read me the entire chapter on the tragic death of the six-year-old child in his new book *Dombey and Son*. What a very droll man he was.

In the 1970s, the United States Defense Department scrapped the use of over 450 computer programming languages and replaced them all with a single object-oriented language. They named it Ada, after me of course. In 2009 the second Tuesday of October was declared Ada Lovelace Day with the aim of creating new role models for girls and women in technology. In November 2015 all British passports were updated to feature my portrait embedded in their pages, which was highly amusing. However, since the abomination known as Brexit, my decorative services have no longer been required in such documents. Your loss, dear reader. Your loss.

And now I shall take my leave of you and make way for the next ghost, as I remain here at rest and in some comfort, lying between two Frenchmen.

Ada Lovelace, 1836, pregnant with her first child.
Daguerrotype image, photographer unknown,
Public domain.

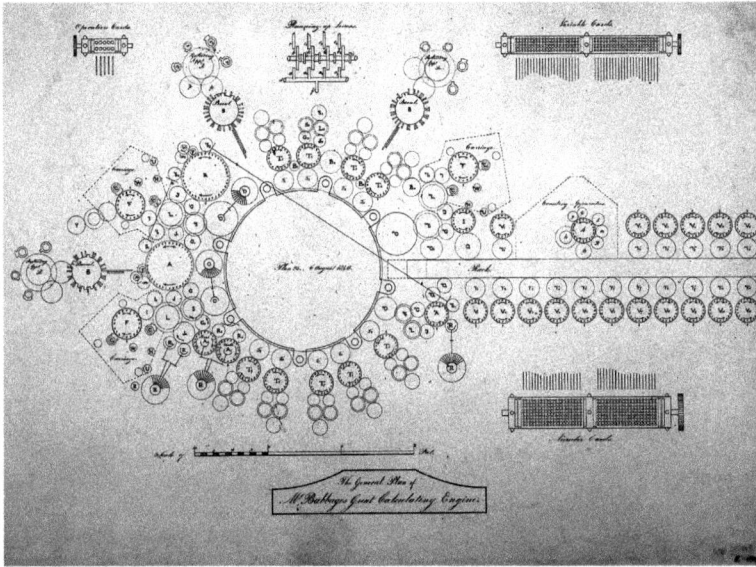

'The General Plan of Mr. Babbage's Great Calculating Engine'
1840.
With acknowledgement and thanks to The Science Museum, London.
Reference BAB/A/089. Open Access for publication.

The Third Ghost

Édouard-Léon Scott de Martinville, 1817-1879

Recorded Sound, 1857

N o matter what technology may evolve behind the scenes, it is my considered opinion that there are only three components which matter to us, the gamers. These are the gameplay itself, also the images that convey that gameplay and finally the sound generated by the gameplay. It is the sound element that was always of interest to me. Since the dawn of time, games have been accompanied by sound, from the cry of *échec et mat* in a game of chess to the pathetic gloop-gloop noises in your electric arcade machines like *Asteroids* and *Space Invaders*.

I am the ghost of Édouard-Léon Scott de Martinville, I was twice married and father of six. I was a printer and seller of books, and it was my avowed intention not only to create a mechanical ear, but to enable my creation to record any sound that it heard, especially the sound of human speech. My inspiration came when I was a young man and the newly invented miracle of photography captured my imagination. But those camera images of my youth were static, as if a brief moment in time had been frozen, whereas I believed that if time was to be captured at all then it must be captured in a sequence or a loop, and I knew that just like the moving image all sound was a continuous flow of signals.

In 1849 I compiled a history of stenography, which is sometimes called shorthand, and I traced the various methods of recording speech and conversations in such a continuous flow without omission. But to my mind using shorthand for speech was like using a chisel to etch an engraving. There was no nuance, no subtlety, no tonality. If I was to create a mechanical ear then I would need to start from basic principles.

Unfortunately, I was not of independent means and I had to earn a living, which I did by typesetting scientific publications. And so it was that was not until 1853 that I took the first steps in my quest for an answer. One dull morning I was tasked with editing the work of a certain Professor Longet titled *Traité de Physiologie*, and while I was proofreading a set of engravings for his textbook on natural physics I came across the most detailed drawings and diagrams of auditory anatomy. Not just of the human ear itself, but of how it actually functions in dynamic terms. It was then that I determined to build a device for photographing the spoken word.

A spoken word is nothing more than a wave carried through the air, and every sound that can be recorded or sampled or generated is processed by the ear in the same way. To begin, sound waves must first be gathered in the fleshy outer ear and then travel through a narrow passageway of gristle called the ear canal, which leads to a thin membrane called the eardrum. The eardrum vibrates from the incoming sound waves and sends these vibrations to three tiny bones in the middle ear. These bones amplify the sound vibrations and send them to a structure shaped like a little snail, which is filled with fluid in the inner ear. A flexible membrane runs from the beginning to the end of this little snail, splitting it into an upper and lower part. When the vibrations cause the fluid to ripple, a traveling wave forms along the membrane. There are sensory hairs sitting on top of the membrane that ride the wave, and the hairs near the wide end of the snail detect high-pitch sounds, like a mouse squeaking, whereas the hairs closer to the centre of the snail's spiral detect low-pitch sounds, like a guard dog growling in annoyance.

And now for the science. As the hairs move up and down, tiny projections bump against one another and cause the tips to open up, and when this happens chemicals burst in and manufacture an electrical signal. A nerve then carries this electrical signal to the brain, which turns it into a sound that we can recognise and understand. That is how we perceive sound in simple terms, however it was no less than another four years before I was able to mimic this entire auditory process into a mechanical device of my own creation.

I attempted experimentation with all sorts of materials to make my artificial outer ear, and soon found that metals and woods were too rigid and tended to distort the sound with reverberation, whereas felts and rubbers and sponges deadened any sound input. In the end I found that the material named after my own city was not only simple to mould, but it was very cheap and very effective, so I used Plaster of Paris!

Making the artificial eardrum was by far the simplest of the challenges for me to solve, and the clue was in the name itself. I used the finest of flexible membranes, stretched over a little circular frame exactly like a drum head. As for the bones of the middle ear, I devised a series of little hinged levers that could move a stylus to act as a sort of audio pen to mark the sound vibrations onto a surface of glass or wood or paper that I covered in lampblack made from the deposits of sooty oil.

There had already been successful transcriptions of audio frequencies captured by the tips of tuning forks vibrating over blackened glass; indeed the English physicist Thomas Young, known as 'the last man who knew everything', had generated distinct graphics using this method ten years before I was born. But tuning forks were rigid and impractical for my purposes and it was the creation of an effective stylus that was my greatest challenge.

I tried everything from pen nibs to thorns, by way of fish bones, until eventually I realised that the answer had been literally staring me in the face for years. One morning, as I lathered my chin to shave with my badger-bristle brush, I observed the solution to my problem in the mirror. Bristles! An animal bristle is not only flexible, durable and abundant, but it is free. I set about harvesting a variety of sproutings from an array of sources including local dog owners and barbers, but none of them presented me with a bristle that was entirely suitable, until thanks to my local butcher I eventually found the perfect donor in the whisker of a savage wild boar. It is said that you cannot make a silk purse out of a sow's ear, but I certainly found my stylus in the ear of her mate, and I was ready to build my prototype.

My initial execution was nowhere near as sophisticated as the model I later presented to the Académie Française, but I was delighted to discover that it was not too difficult to fashion. I coated the smoothest plate of glass I could find with the thinnest layer of lampblack to use as my medium for recording the audio vibrations. My oversize model of the human ear I have already described, and now I proved that a rigid boar's bristle of between one and two centimetres long was the ideal means to transfer the sound vibrations from the centre the drum membrane to the glass plate. While I spoke into the wide end of my plaster ear trumpet, I employed my own hand to slide the glass plate horizontally between two grooves as the bristle drew a unique sound pattern. When I uttered different vocalisations I observed different patterns being recorded. A plosive actually looked like a plosive, as did a fricative and a vowel. My theory worked in practice!

Unfortunately my mechanical skills were insufficient to fabricate a more sophisticated machine, and I needed a better device by which I could crank a long roll of smooth paper at a constant speed to act as my recording medium, and I also needed the operation to be stable enough to capture a period of continuous speech or music. My butcher told me of a skilled young *fée* who was living on the Île Saint-Louis within sight of Notre Dame, a Prussian craftsman named Karl Koenig who it was said specialised in acoustics. He lived alone and seemed to have few friends, but I found him most amenable and he appeared willing to help me with my invention which I had by then named the Phonautograph.

Herr Koenig not only fabricated a sturdy metal frame for all of my Phonautograph components, but he integrated a perfect hand-crank mechanism and improved the design of my speaking horn. In addition, he made the interaction of my components much easier to finesse, thanks to a series of control wheels with screw-thread adjustments for height and tolerance. Above all, he reduced the size of every element, thereby making my device portable.

On March the 25th in the year 1857 I was granted patent number 17,897/31,470 for my sound recording invention, and as I looked forward to the prospect of riches beyond my wildest dreams I began to plan the construction of a factory to produce Phonautographs by the thousand. I anticipated that every office and academic institution in Paris would see the benefit of recorded sound, and that its success would spread throughout the country and thence beyond its borders. I imagined the world-wide clamour for my portable recorders in the home, where they would be used for family archives, wills and testaments, entertainment and gaming.

But my dreams were ill founded. I only sold a pitiful few of my machines to scientific institutions and audio researchers, and if truth be told, my invention was greeted with wholesale indifference. I had no notion of how to publicise my concept, and as the weeks turned into months I felt crushed by disappointment. I freely admit that I did not profit from my audio invention in the slightest.

And so it was that I returned to a life of dealing in books, prints and photographs at 9 Rue Vivienne in Paris, and it was that intellectual thief Thomas Edison who went down in the history books as the first to record the human voice twenty years later. His Phonograph device was almost identical to my Phonautograph, apart from the recording medium which was made of tin foil, and the fact that he could reverse the head of the recording device so that it played back through the ear trumpet. So much for the history books, but I am still the ghost in every recording machine ever made, no matter whose name it bears on the patent. So let me put the record straight here and now and endorse the true history of events.

It was a Monday morning, the ninth day of April 1860, when I recorded myself singing the old folk song *Au Clair de la Lune* on an updated model of my Phonautograph. I used a roll of smooth paper which could cope with up to thirty seconds of continuous sound. The recording was witnessed by a small number of members of the Société d'Encouragement pour l'Industrie Nationale, and was duly filed in a drawer along with my handwritten notes of accreditation, where it languished for 151 years at the Académie des Sciences.

In 2008, a group of historians and audio enthusiasts from the United States of America were trawling through ancient ledgers when they not only found my original patent but they discovered a number of my recordings in the same archive. They took the paper trace of *Au Clair de la Lune* and had it digitised at the Lawrence Berkeley National Laboratory in the State of California. They then linked a standard optical scanner using image-to-sound conversion software and they played back the ghost of my voice through a common personal computer. At first they believed the folk song they could hear had been sung by a child, until they realised they were playing it at double speed, adjusted the tempo and heard my communication from the past. They later wrote a clever little computer routine to stabilise the fluttering caused by my uneven cranking of the recording handle, and they released my recording via your Internet global communication system where you may hear it today.

You see, I really have been observing the progress made with all your computing and gaming devices since I died, and quite frankly, after due consideration, you are more than welcome to stick them where the sun does not shine.

Édouard-Léon Scott de Martinville
engraving by Louis Figuier, 1891, public domain

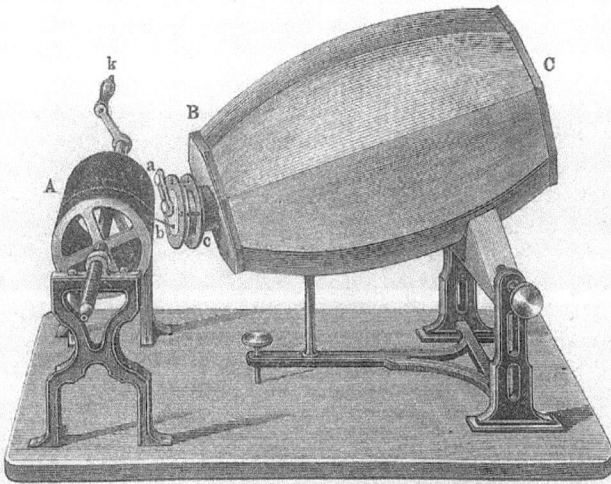

The Phonautograph
engraving by Francis Rolt-Wheeler, 1909, public domain

The Fourth Ghost

Charles-Émile Reynaud, 1844-1918

The Gamification of Animation, 1888

Y es, we do talk with one another, you know, we ghosts in the machine. We discuss our ideas and inventions, and we keep abreast of modern times when it comes to our legacies. Naturally I mostly converse with my other Francophones, which is understandable, *n'est-ce pas*, but I can assure you that of all the ghosts who merit a chapter in this publication, I am by far the most important. It was I who dealt purely with the creation of illusion, of phantoms, of ghostly apparitions and cinematic trickery, and it was I who first created everything that you recognise as the components of your modern day animated gaming.

And not only animation. I gave you cinematic cuts and I introduced compositing. And who was it who invented multi-layered backgrounds? Preprogrammed sprites? Stop-motion? User-controlled characters? Synchronised audio? Storyboarding? Vector graphics? Parallax scrolling? Random pathways? Action replays? I am aware that all of these elements may have gained prominence in 1980s video-gaming, but my dear friends it was I who first developed them one hundred years beforehand, and it was I who entertained over half a million souls with them before the twentieth century was even born let alone the twenty-first. Permit me to introduce myself. I am Charles-Émile Reynaud, inventor, showman and undeniable genius. Welcome to the show. Abracadabra!

I was born in Paris in the same week that the first public electric lighting illuminated our Place de la Concorde, at the beginning of December in the year 1844. An auspicious occasion, and an omen of the illuminated spectacles that I would one day bring to my adoring audiences. Brutus, my dear Papa, was a talented engineer and a fine engraver. Marie-Caroline, my dear Mama, was an exceptional artist, and she had the privilege of staying at home to educate me in the skills of painting and engraving. I was, of course, an insufferable child prodigy, and of all my insufferable childish proclivities what I excelled at most of all was the creative manipulation of my toy theatre.

My little theatre was a table-top affair, a model made in Milan of brightly printed cardboard. My favourite drama was called *La Pleine Mer*, or in English *The Open Sea*. It had been in my family for many years, and was a little scuffed and dog-eared, but to me it was magical. The backdrop was the wide ocean, the middle flats were a series of moveable waves that grew from a modest swell to great foaming breakers, and the foreground was of a coral island. As well as mighty sailing ships and native canoes, there were all sorts of cardboard characters and props attached to little sticks, that I could slide in and out of the stage between the flats. I remember most clearly that there was a whale and a drowning sailor, and there were all manor of savages, as well as a mermaid, a shark with bloody teeth and some kind of green monster with long tentacles. And I also had a booklet which contained several melodramas for reading aloud, and which were supposed to give me inspiration. But I never really bothered with them. I much preferred to create my own precocious dramatic productions.

I would illuminate my miniature stage with strategically placed candlelight, and I only scorched my sets on very rare occasions. I used little mirrors to create moving reflections, and sometimes I would add sound effects using a music box or the percussion of a spoon banged on a metal tray. My mother always showed modest interest in my efforts, but my father had limited time to enjoy the fruits of my creativity because he had to be engaged in his work. However my parents were good enough to allow me to invite other children into the home in order to witness my theatrical flair.

And then, one momentous day when I was about nine or ten years of age, a life-changing revelation came to me. I concluded that I could charge the members of my juvenile audience the modest sum of one copper centime for the privilege of enjoying one of my splendid productions. Oh how I enjoyed collecting their lovely little coins, with Lady Liberty's head gazing into the distance, stage left. I saved up those coins in a small wooden box, until I had amassed enough to purchase some glass slides and some miniature bottles of aniline ink with which to paint magic lantern scenes.

Naturally, I was determined to create my own backdrops and my own little characters on sticks, but my early experiments were neither particularly professional nor were they robust. However, they improved as I transitioned through adolescence, and as soon as I was of an age to spread my wings my father agreed to apprentice me to a printmaker of his acquaintance. And so it was that I took my first professional steps on the pathway to designer glory.

A mechanical device known as the *zoetrope* had been introduced by an American gentleman named Milton Bradley. I would have been twenty-two years old at the time, and it set my mind racing. For those of you who are not familiar with Greek, the word *zoe* means life, and the word *tropos* is

35

associated with the motion of turning. His device was intended as a child's toy that produced moving images by viewing a series of static images through little slits in a revolving drum, and where Mr Bradley made his fortune was not only to sell his miniature carousels but also to offer a series of replaceable film strips for loading inside them. A man after my own heart, and a man I very much wished to emulate.

The principle that Bradley used was by no means original. I had read of an earthenware bowl from ancient Persia that depicts the sequence of a jumping goat, and which is at least three thousand years old. If the bowl is illuminated to one side by a lamp, and the illumination is interrupted by flapping a hand between the lamp and the spinning bowl, then the illusion of animation is created. And one hundred years before Christ, there was a Chinese engineer called Ding Huan who created a hollow lamp with a band of birdlike images which animated when the heat of the lamp caused the band to rotate and the birds to fly. And when Henrietta Maria was Queen of England, she was entertained by a similar device consisting of a glass cylinder inside of which was a quartet of images drawn onto cards held on a four-spoked wheel, and which revolved when placed in a beam of sunlight.

However, it was left to a man of my acumen and commercial ambition to turn these principles into gold, and I began serious experimentation not only on the principles of the moving image, but on how the human eye can be deluded into perceiving such motion.

I filed the patent for my genius in December 1888, the year Monsieur Eiffel built his great tower, the year Vincent Van Gogh cut off his own ear and presented it to the nearest brothel, and the year Louis Le Prince captured the first motion picture on a strip of film. Unlike Monsieur Le Prince's passive and invariable image, my moving images could be manipulated in an infinite variety of ways, and in their wisdom the Patent Office recognised the originality of all aspects of my new technology for mass entertainment, which I called the *Théâtre Optique*.

My patent allowed for a roll of film to be of indefinite length and made of any material whether transparent or opaque. Indeed, I much preferred images on brightly lit opaque media, which could be bounced off mirrors and projected, and I will tell you more about my harnessing of mirrors in a short while. My entertainment images could be photographic, or printed or hand drawn, and in my demonstration model I provided a fifty metre horizontal film strip of seven hundred transparent images which I sequenced against dark backgrounds. I hand-painted them myself onto square gelatin plates each the size of my hand. I coated the edges of every plate with shellac and framed them in a strip of cardboard linked by bands of fabric and attached with split pins. I used black leader-tape at the beginning and at the end, where introductions and credits could be cut out or printed, and I punched a small oblong perforation in the centre between each image, which engaged with metal pins protruding from a central rotating wheel. It was this calibrated wheel that transferred my sequence of images between two large copper spools to hold and receive the film strip. And now comes the magic.

The film was guided with exact precision by a series of pinch rollers to pass in front of a projection lantern. Each image was projected in turn towards one of thirty-six mirrors in the middle of the rotating wheel, and each image was reflected once again through a focussing lens towards another moveable mirror. These mirrors were adjusted and tilted so as to project moving characters and objects to any desired position within the background image on a screen, and my changeable backgrounds were then projected by a second magic lantern using glass plates. Sequences were run by a hand-crank at any speed, forwards or backwards, and repeated as often as the narrative required. I called my device the Praxinoscope, and I included synchronised music and sound effects triggered by metal tabs on the film strip to activate electromagnets for music boxes, percussion, buzzers and bells.

Within a year of my patent being granted, I commercialised my Théâtre Optique in several versions for home use as well as theatrical shows, and I made copies of my film strips available to anyone who would pay. Of course, I revelled in exploiting my own skills of vocal narration and piano accompaniment to enhance my productions, and I soon set myself up in the Musée Grévin, the wax museum on the banks of the Seine, which emulated Madame Tussauds in London for *pantomimes lumineuses*. Ah what a joy it was to captivate my audiences as I gamified the entertainment to their cries of *encore*!

Over a period of eight years, I performed in excess of 12,800 shows and relieved more than 500,000 customers of their money. My most popular production was *Autour d'une cabine ou Mésaventures d'un copurchic aux bains de mer*, which may be translated as 'Around a Cabin, or the Misadventures of a Swell at the Seaside'. Yes, yes, I know, it harks back to the seascapes of the toy theatre of my childhood, but why not? A true genius does not so much create as adapt. Here is what I termed the screenplay.

After the opening title credits, a colourful seascape depicts a sandy beach with a rocky crag offshore, a pair of beach huts and a diving board. A pretty young woman appears and leaps off the diving board into the sea. She emerges as a fat man dithers about, hesitating to take the plunge. The young woman then comes up behind him on the diving board and unceremoniously pushes him into the water before jumping off again to join him. After floundering about the man bobs off and the woman returns to shore. Then she plays around with a little spaniel and picks the dog up, but it jumps out of her arms. Suddenly a sinister man leaps out and scares her so much she faints, but he apologises and helps her to her feet. She runs off to her beach hut to get changed, but the sinister man spies on her in a state of undress. But what is this? A hero comes out of the other beach hut, kicks the peeping tom up the *derrière* and chases him away. When the pretty lady emerges from her own beach hut she has the overwhelming urge to take her clothes off again and invites the hero to join her in the sea, where they mess about above and beneath the water before swimming out of the scene. Finally a boat appears with an old man on board, who unfurls the sail to reveal the words *La représentation est terminée*, or in the parlance of the Looney Tunes and adopted by Porky Pig in a later era, "That's all folks."

Which in my case, is not at all true, because all of the action was user-controlled and the gameplay was as variable as the imagination allowed. I had not only invented interactive gameplay, but also made a fortune out of it. Unfortunately, the same cannot be said of the next ghost in the machine.

Charles-Émile Reynaud, 1888
photographer unknown, public domain

image from *Autour d'une cabine*, 1894
by Charles-Émile Reynaud, 1894, public domain.

The Fifth Ghost

Paul Otlet 1868-1944

The Internet, 1934

A nd exactly how many of you are there? How many of you are out there playing your videogames and your esports and living out your virtual lives as avatars and virtual combatants? How many of you are there, absorbed in your screens, tapping your buttons, gaming, gaming, gaming? Quantify yourselves.

They say you are forty per cent of the world's population. Is that three and a half billion? Is it more by now? Whatever the truth of the matter, there would be none of you at all if it had not been for what you refer to as the Internet. And I wonder how many of you know who invented your internet, who designed it, who actually built it. Was it Tim Berners-Lee? No, it was not he. Was it Vinton Cerf and Bob Kahn? Never. Was it Louis Pouzin, Hubert Zimmermann or Peter Kirstein? *Non, niet, nein.* They are all parvenus. Before any of them could pucker their lips to suckle at their mother's teat it was I, a Belgian with a beard, Paul Marie

Ghislain Otlet, who conceived your Internet. *C'était moi!*

Although my work has been forgotten, it has been most affirming to be introduced to my fellow ghosts, although not entirely unexpected. I knew of Jacquard's data cards of course, everybody did, and I have always been familiar with the brilliant theories of Ada Lovelace having read her notes avidly while I was still at school at the Lycée Louis-le-Grand. I remember telling my tutor that her command of French was remarkably good. And when I was a young man in Paris I also enjoyed several performances at the *Théâtre Optique* given by Monsieur Reynaud, but I was unaware of Scott de Martinville's achievements and had believed that it was Herr Berliner who endowed humanity with the microphone and recorded sound. My apologies to de Martinville, but such is the fate of a forgotten pioneer, as of course my own fate attests.

By the time I had developed my own theories, both cinema and sound recording were commonplace, as was telephony and wireless broadcasting. My revolutionary concept was to harness all such technology and create a universal artificial brain for the common good, for information and for entertainment. I will now tell you how I achieved it.

I am a Belgian. My father was a megalomaniac captain of industry, and my childhood was privileged but lonely. I hated it all, except for the books in our own library. When I was ten years old I enlisted my younger brother to help me create an index of ideas that I called The Company of Useful Knowledge. My life's work had begun, although I did not publish my first account of a universal library until I was 23 years old and a qualified lawyer. In 1891 I began with a rallying call to systematically classify all sources of information as follows.

"Stuff that has already been written and thought provides the basic materials. It is, therefore, quite natural to make a systematic inventory of everything - both historical and contemporary, a catalogue of everything in books, brochures, and journals, arranged systematically. This work can begin at once. It can fall into two series. One series is a retrospective of all knowledge assembled to date, and the other series is of all new published knowledge to be updated month by month.

What I propose is that we need a standard format index, and reduce the data to four elements: the facts, the interpretation of facts, the statistics and the sources. The data can then be brought together and re-arranged to answer any question that anyone can pose. The various parts of any book, or article, or lecture can be easily reduced to these four elements, not along the lines of the special plan of any particular publication, but according to the index appropriate to each element.

This systematic recording of facts, statistical data and interpretations need only be undertaken by a few individuals who will create a kind of artificial brain by means of cards containing actual information, notes and references."

By the year 1906 I had revolutionised my concept of data storage by setting up a workable microfilm system, and it was in that year that I published *Les Aspects du Livre*, in which I predicted mobile networks a full eighty years before the real thing.

"Tomorrow, telephony will be wireless, just like telegraphy. Nobody can stop me from believing this. We will witness a new transformation of the book. Everyone will carry a tiny little handset in his or her pocket, which will be tuned with the turn of a dial to the unique wavelength transmitted by each information-emitting-centre."

So much for the theory. I now set about putting theory into practice. I was fortunate to have a friend and colleague who was not only rich and famous, but knew a great many others who were also rich and famous. His name was Henri La Fontaine, and one day he would go on to win the Nobel Peace Prize. He shared my vision of a global artificial brain as a repository for all knowledge to be harnessed for international peace and cooperation, but I was dreadful at doing business and it was Henri who always raised the money.

He wheedled and cajoled everyone he knew who had their finger in the Belgian financial pie, and on the 23rd of April 1910 The Brussels International Exposition opened and it ran until the first day of November. Immediately after it closed I was given permission to combine an international library, an international museum, an international university, a central hub for official international institutions and my ever-expanding card-index data service, and soon all of these services and institutes were housed at the exhibition site. The cost of setting everything up was a massive half a million francs, paid for by the Belgian Government, and it was then that I named our project the *Mundaneum*.

My new data hub was on a scale far beyond my wildest dreams. As well as the grand entrance hall and wide circulation areas, the layout ran to eighteen rooms for administration offices, four great auditoriums, five bibliographic centres, another nine rooms for an international library, thirty-five galleries for international museums and seven university study hubs. The funding also allowed me to include two information centres, two massive chambers for the data-processing of sixteen million searchable cards, a dedicated telephone and telegraph complex, a restaurant and a smoking room. This is not a record of speculation, dear reader of the Internet age, this is a record of what I actually assembled, fully operational, fully staffed, and open to the public for subscription services.

But the clouds of war began to gather on the European horizon. Prospective new investors got cold feet and I failed to foresee that this was the shape of things to come. From that day on, restrictions on funding meant that the *Mundaneum* would never expand again, and in the real world, my dream was over. Meanwhile, in my own private world I simply failed to wake up to the reality until it was far too late. The Belgian economy was shattered by the first war, and twenty years later the great Depression struck, which was catastrophic for my project. By 1934, with all funding gone, I published one last appeal for the world to embrace my ideas and use technology for peace and not war. This is what I said:

"We are where we are, and now what we must do is to move on. And what we must do is to assemble a collection of machines which can perform the following operations, simultaneously or sequentially. What I am talking about is machines that can deliver seven individual operations which must be performed together. Let me list them for you.

Operation number One - the transformation of sound into writing.

Operation number Two - the reproduction of this writing into as many copies as are needed.

Operation number Three - the creation of data in such a way that each item of information has its own identity, and in its relationships with other items comprising any collection of data, can be retrieved as necessary.

Operation number Four - a classification reference number assigned to each specific item of information.

Operation number Five - the automatic classification and filing of this data by machine.

Operation number Six - the automatic retrieval of data for consultation, presented either direct to the enquirer or via machine, enabling typed additions to be made.

And finally, operation number Seven - the mechanical manipulation at will of all the listed items of information, in order to obtain new combinations of facts, new relationships of ideas, and new operations carried out with the help of numeric code.

The technology fulfilling these seven requirements will create a mechanical collective brain.

All information must be condensed so that it can be contained on a personal desk, within hand's reach, and indexed in such a way as to ensure maximum accessibility.

In this case, the world described in the entirety of all knowledge will be within everyone's grasp. A Universal Book.

The Universal Book created from all books will become an annex to the brain, a substratum of memory, an external mechanism and instrument of the mind, but so close to it, so apt to its use that it will truly be an extension of humans.

Man will no longer need documentation to become an omniscient being like God himself. A less ultimate degree will create instrumentation acting across any distance which simultaneously combines radio broadcasts, x-rays, cinema and microscopic photography.

All the things in the universe and all those of man will be registered remotely as they are produced. Thus the reflected image of the world will be established - the world's complete memory, its true duplicate.

Anyone will be able to consult information remotely from afar, expanded or limited to the desired subject, projected on their individual screen.

Thus, in their armchair at home or in their place of work, anyone will be able to contemplate the whole of creation, or any part of it."

While my *Mundaneum* data hub was left to rot, I compressed my entire life's work into one huge book, my *Traité de Documentation*, and it is there I included a pair of hand-drawn sketches that are as important as the entire treatise. On two sheets of paper, catalogued as Documents 8440 and 8441 by P. Otlet for the *Encyclopedia Universalis Mundaneum* and headed *Documentation et Telecommunication*, I drew a series of frames set out like a graphic novel with my captions in capital letters.

Frame 1 shows a matrix of mixed media combining telephones, radios, audio data discs, film and television, and how these are combined to allow live conference calls.

Frame 2 shows a number of subscribers in remote locations, each wearing a set of headphones and each connected to a telephone terminal. Their telephones are linked to a central data hub. The caption reads, "National or international committee meeting. Subscribers can listen and speak and are connected to one another through a hub at the central office."

The caption for Frame 3 reads, "Congress Session, held in the presence of members who are on remote sites." The illustration is of a large number of users in Brussels seated in front of a wide-screen presentation linked by hard wire and wirelessly. The split-screen shows the identical image as the one shown in Brussels being viewed by remote groups of subscribers in distant locations including Paris.

In Frame 4 there is a device sitting on a desk. The device looks exactly like your modern flat-screens with a letterbox aspect ratio. It is wireless and it is shown scanning a document. There is a television connected to the device which displays the identical image of the scanned document. The caption reads, "Transmission of document graphics by television screen."

Frame 5 expands the range of media, and shows more than one scanner linked to telephones and televisions and delivering audio from disc and images from film of a recorded video. The accompanying text says, "Stored data (on disc or film) sent by telephone or television."

Frame 6 occupies the whole width of the page, and is heavily annotated. Top-left is a series of catalogued data labelled books, films, audio discs and 'objects'. Next is the entire content of the *Mundaneum* data storage hub miniaturised to fit on two tables and mechanically linked to a series of scanners. The extracted data is then transmitted through a screening unit and delivered to remote television screens. My hand-written annotations are too long to fit in the panel and get squashed into the bottom of the space, showing the speed at which I was working. They read as follows.

"(A) Documentation consisting of collections and catalogs will duplicate the entire content of the *Mundaneum*.

(B and C) Here, machines will help with complementary operations, analysis and synthesis, needed to deliver whatever encyclopaedic knowledge the user demands.

(D) The requested elements will be mechanically

extracted.

(E) Transmitters will launch them into the universal network from where they will be received by workstations."

You can only agree that this single document is enough justification for me to be recognised as the inventor of the Internet, which now allows your gaming to be of a global nature, and limitless in its scope.

I know that in your time I am a forgotten man, and I can assure you that in my time I was also sidelined and then unrecognised. I remember that one afternoon, after I delivered my sketch designs for the technology of the future, I took myself off to the cinema to see what the future of entertainment would one day provide, a future of gambling, violence and pornography which is the mainstay of your Internet age. I went to watch a movie called *Ecstasy*, starring a young Austrian girl called Hedy Lamarr. It had just been banned in Nazi Germany, which was a good enough reason for me to go and watch it in protest against their disgusting and dangerous beliefs. I did not like the movie very much, but my wife did.

Paul Otlet, Mundaneum 20th anniversary portrait, 1934
photographer unknown, Mundaneum Wallonia-Brussels Federation
collection research archives. Public Domain.

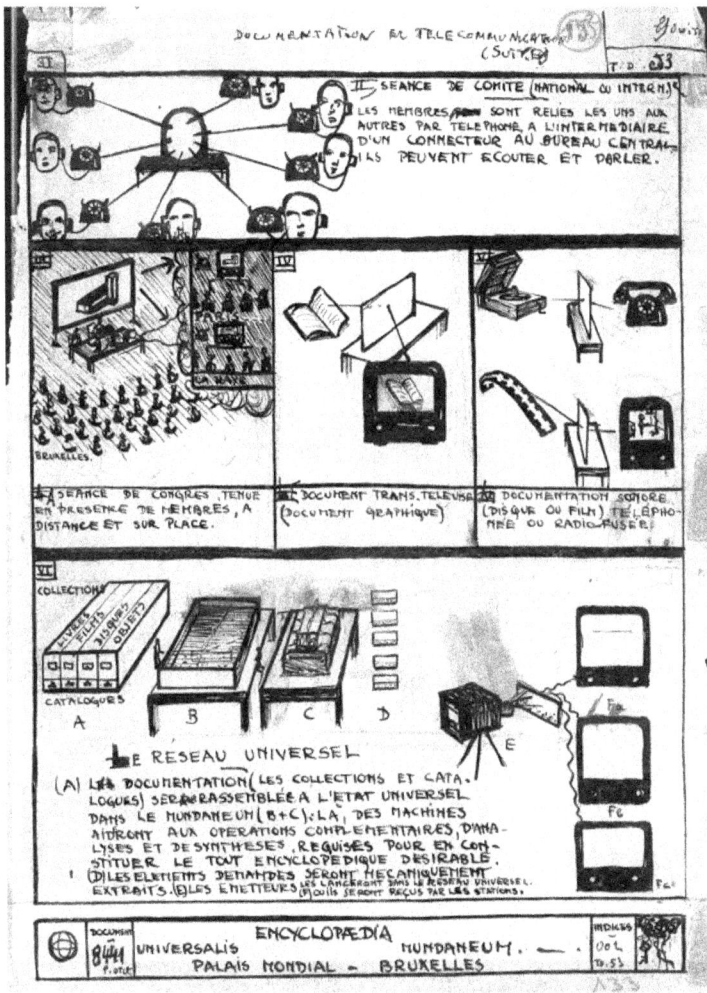

Document 8441, sketch design for the Internet, 1934
Paul Otlet. Mundaneum Wallonia-Brussels Federation collection research archives and European Commission for Culture and Creativity.
Public Domain.

The Sixth Ghost

Hedy Lamarr 1914-2000

Wi-Fi, 1941

D o you think I am beautiful? Paul Otlet thought so. Do you agree with all those who named me the most beautiful woman in the world? And do I even care what you think? No, I do not even care. I know who I am, I know what I am, and I know what I was.

I was born Hedwig Eva Maria Kiesler in the Vienna of 1914, and I do not wish to be remembered for being the accredited inspiration for Snow White, or Cat Woman, or for my six marriages, or for faking the first female orgasm ever shown in a movie, and you know something Monsieur Otlet, maybe I didn't fake it at all. No, I want you to remember me for creating all the possibilities for your own pleasures. I want you to remember me for giving you Wi-Fi, Bluetooth, cordless phones, GPS, surveillance drones and online gaming. And if you want, you can also remember me for giving you carbonated drinks, the jet aircraft wing, modern traffic lights, the fluorescent dog collar, and guided missile control. But I guess you are here for the gaming and not all my other stuff.

I never wanted to be a movie star. I wanted to be an inventor. My heroes were Joseph Jacquard for turning a music box into a computer, and Ada Lovelace for explaining random number generation, and of course Paul Otlet for giving me the notion of wireless data communication. Mind you, I didn't need any of them to teach me how to think. I disassembled and reassembled our family music box at the age of five, and I could speak four languages by the time I was ten. My family was rich, they were bankers, they were Jewish, and they could not control me in the slightest.

I ran away to Berlin aged sixteen and enrolled at the great Max Reinhardt's drama school. But I soon realised that a theatre stage wasn't big enough for me. I had set my sights firmly on the magic that was the silver screen. With a face and a brain like mine the movies were a pushover, but it was my eighteen year-old naked body that brought me world fame. The film in which I made my movie debut was called *Ecstasy* and it had the honour of being banned in Germany, and denounced as "obscene, immoral and dangerously indecent" in the USA, and damned to hell by Pope Pius XI. How could I possibly fail?

Soon after, I changed my name from Hedy Kiesler to the much more glamorous Hedy Lamarr, and temporarily gave up the movies to marry an Austrian arms baron called Fritz. I didn't really like him, but he was extremely rich. It was not so much that I wanted to give up the movies, it was more to do with the fact that my husband tried to destroy every print of *Ecstasy* he could find, and then had the unmitigated audacity to try and imprison me in order to prevent me flaunting myself on screen again. What a prick.

Of course I left him, but not until after I had meekly attended his countless dinner parties and listened to all those detailed discussions about innovations in the arms trade with the other death-mongers. I may have listened in silence and appeared to be bored by it all, but I did not forget a word.

Obviously I headed for Hollywood as soon as I dumped him, which is where I got back into the movie business and took my pick of its most desirable men. Among them was Howard Hughes, one of the richest, weirdest and most influential men in the world, and heavily into media, aerospace and investment. He really was the Elon Musk of his day, but I'll say this for him; he uncorked my scientific mind that had been bottled up far too long. In fact he set me up with a miniature lab so I could work on my innovations and theories when I wasn't needed on the film set.

Howard gave me free range at his aircraft factories, and it was clear that I could hold my own with the scientists who worked for him. We all knew there was a war coming over in Europe, and my favourite project was one where he wanted to build the fastest plane ever so he could sell it to the US military. The pathway to creating this seemed obvious to me, so I took myself off and researched the aerodynamics of the fastest bird in the sky along with the aquadynamics of the fastest fish in the sea, and I combined the two designs to create a new airlift and wing system for his prototype. His comment on receiving my results went down in history: "She's a ****ing genius." I'm not quite sure if his double-meaning was intentional, but improving scientific norms came naturally to me, and if that is genius then I am happy to accept the accolade.

A couple of years before the USA entered the Second World War, I had been taken under the polished wing of the head of MGM studios Louis B Meyer, and I was an A-list celebrity again. That was when I met the film-writer, musician and mechanical inventor George Antheil. It was at a dinner party, and I remember that our first conversation was about Ada Lovelace and Charles Babbage meeting under exactly the same circumstances. To annoy several other guests we spoke in our original family language of German. *Was für ein Lachen!*

I told him about my invention of a tablet that made Coca-Cola when you dropped it in a glass of water. He told me about his composition for a robot orchestra of sixteen player-pianos, a siren and three airplane propellors. Then I told him about my aircraft design for Howard. And then he name-dropped Aaron Copland, Cecil B DeMille, Ernest Hemingway, Igor Stravinski, Ezra Pound and Jean Cocteau. It was like an arms race of self-satisfaction, so naturally we ended up talking about sex.

George Antheil considered himself to be an expert on the subjects of female biology, hormones and intimate secretions, and he was working on a theory about how to determine the availability of a woman based on her glandular readings. As the Most Beautiful Woman In The World it seemed obvious for me to ask him the one unsolved question that had been on my mind since I made *Ecstasy*. Which was how to enhance my mammaries. He considered the attributes of my breasts for a long time then suggested a course of glandular extracts as we discussed size, shape, weight, mobility and dynamics. Which is what led us on to torpedoes. I swear on my life all this is true. At least I would swear on my life if I wasn't a ghost.

Antheil recalled our conversation in one of his published pieces like this, "Hedy said she did not feel comfortable, sitting there in Hollywood and making lots of money when things were in such a state in Europe. After her marriage to Fritz Mandl, she had a knowledge of munitions and weaponry that could prove beneficial. And so, we began to tinker with ideas about how to combat the axis powers and help defeat the Nazis."

I was twenty-six years old and world-famous as a dumb little movie actress, but I what I really wanted was to be taken seriously by the Government just as I had been by Howard Hughes and his technicians. George knew how to synchronise player-pianos electronically and had taught himself how to program. I knew how to invent the weapons of war and had taught myself about radio control. And so we

58

went to work.

First I set about deciding what the war effort needed most, and reckoned that ever since the end of the Battle of Britain the greatest danger no longer came from the air, but from the sea. I had attended plenty of arms deals acting as arm-candy for my first husband Fritz, and I knew for a fact that what the Navy wanted was a way to guide a torpedo onto its target as is streaked under the water. I also knew that radio control had been tried, and that it had failed because a radio frequency is easy to jam, which sends the torpedo haywire.

In George's 1924 film-score *Ballet Mécanique*, he had synchronised the start time of identical player pianos with identical piano rolls. So I wondered what the result would be if we treated different radio frequencies like the different notes in those piano rolls, and then miniaturised the mechanism. In that way the conductor of the mechanical orchestra would become the radio signal sender, and the instrumentalists of the mechanical orchestra would become the radio signal receiver. All the time that the sender and receiver were synchronised then the radio control would keep working, no matter how fast frequencies got swapped. And if the frequencies were swapped fast enough then it would be impossible for the enemy to jam them. I gave this idea the name Frequency Hopping.

I submitted my idea to the National Inventors Council just before Christmas 1940, and they recommended a professor of electrical engineering at Caltech to help with a demonstration of the system. In 1941 I called in my lawyers to draft me a patent application, and soon after that the Japanese went and bombed Pearl Harbour and America was in the War. It took until the August of 1942 for me to be granted US Patent number 2,292,387 for my invention of a 'secret and secure radio-controlled communications system', and I made damn sure it was granted under my legal name of Hedy Keisler, to stop any of my ex-husbands cashing in.

George and I took it to the US Navy and demonstrated

to them how it would help defeat the enemy. And you know what they did? They gave us the finger, and told me I'd be better off using my celebrity and looks to help sell war bonds. Stupid bastards. We never made a cent out of the system, and my patent expired in 1960. That was forty years before the Institute of Electrical and Electronic Engineers named my system Wi-Fi and it got released to consumers to change the world of communications and gaming.

Back in 1942 I teamed up with a sailor by the name of Eddie Rhodes, and we toured the land to raise money for the war effort. At each rally Eddie would be planted in the crowd and I would go through the pretence of selecting him as an ordinary serviceman to call up on stage. Then we'd flirt a little and he'd beg me for a kiss. I'd ask the crowd if I should satisfy his desire, and the crowd would yell hell yes. At which point I'd agree, but only if enough people bought war bonds. They put their hands in their pockets, and I put my hands in Eddie's, then I would kiss him like a pro and send him off back into the crowd. And after that we'd head off to the next rally.

I guess I helped win the war after all, but it took another woman to help us change the modern world of computing and gaming. She was in the Navy just like my Eddie, but unlike him she reached the lofty rank of Rear Admiral. Let me hand you over to Grace Hopper to continue our story in the next chapter.

Meanwhile, in the second decade of the twenty-first century, I was inducted into the National Inventors Hall of Fame fourteen years after I died. Too little, too late.

I believe your world isn't getting any easier. With all your new inventions I believe that people are being pushed more and getting hurried more. That's not the right way. You need time for everything. Time to work, time to rest, and time to play. Hope and curiosity about the future is far better than guarantees. The unknown was always so attractive to me, that's the way I was, and that's the way I will always be. And now answer me this, do you think I am beautiful?

Hedy Lamarr, 1939.
Los Angeles Times, CC BY 4.0 creativecommons.org/license
Wikimedia Commons, with kind permission for use in print.

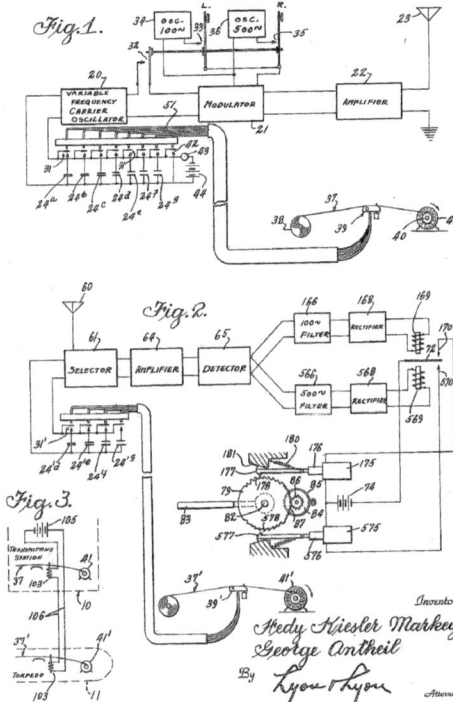

Aug. 11, 1942.   H. K. MARKEY ET AL   2,292,387

SECRET COMMUNICATION SYSTEM

Filed June 10, 1941   2 Sheets-Sheet 1

US Patent 2,292,387, 1942, for 'frequency-hopping'.
Granted to Hedy Lamarr under her married name.
Reproduced under the US Department of Labor expiry rules, Public Domain.

The Seventh Ghost

Grace Hopper 1906-1992

Machine Code, 1946

I am Doctor Grace Brewster Murray Hopper, Rear Admiral US Navy, and you can call me Ma'am. I am not so much a ghost in the machine as I am the ghost in the code of every computer game you have ever played, and I'm telling you this with all authority because I literally wrote the book. They used to call me Amazing Grace, and you can make up your own mind about that after I've told you my story.

My Scots father was an insurance broker, and he was a great one for pattern recognition and numbers. My Dutch mother was the daughter of a high-flyer New York civil engineer, she loved mathematics and she passed that love on to me. I was born the eldest of three in 1906.

Girls of my era were conditioned to be deferential and modest, and they played house with miniature kitchens and cutesy dolls. When they gave me a dollhouse I went and built an elevator for it. It's no surprise to me that the other women ghosts in this book demonstrated their quest for knowledge very early in life, usually by taking apart mechanical devices like music boxes. And I was no exception, although I was quite exceptional.

When I was no older than seven I took my parents' alarm clock apart, but I couldn't fathom how or why it worked. It seemed obvious to me that the way to figure that out was not to try and put it back together again but to dismantle every other clock in the house.

I guess you would have called me a tomboy, and I was no stranger to exploring the outdoors or playing contact sports. And then when I was eight my father had to have both his legs amputated. I remember he was so brave about it, and I never heard him complain or feel sorry for himself. Maybe that was the beginning of my confidence to face any challenge head on. Maybe. Anyway, both my parents encouraged me to get the best education possible so I could be self-reliant and support myself. I never looked back, and I will always thank them for it.

After private school in New York, I went to Vassar as soon as I reached seventeen, which was where they had pioneered women's education for generations. We thought of ourselves as a breed apart. We were programmed to be independent in our thoughts and we were taught to always seek out the source in search of our answers. After I graduated from there with honours in physics and maths it was off to Yale to study for my Masters and on to my doctorate.

In 1930 I returned to Vassar, not as a student but as a math professor. That's where I met Vincent Hopper, who was professor of literature, and we married the same year. It wasn't exactly love, in fact it wasn't exactly anything, and to cut to the chase, it didn't work out. We separated before the War and we divorced after it. I kept nothing of his except his name, and from 1934 onwards I devoted my entire working life to mathematics, computers and programming. I devoted a lot of my non-working life to alcohol, but we'll come to that later. Got it? Good. Let's move on.

In 1942 I volunteered to join the War effort as soon as I could. But I got rejected, not just for being too old but also for being a shrimp. But as I say, I was a Vassar girl and I wouldn't take no for an answer, and the next year they granted me a waiver to join the US Women's Naval Reserve. Vassar gave me leave of absence and I sailed through sixty days intensive training in Northampton at the Midshipman School for Women, Smith College. As soon as I got my commission as Lieutenant Junior Grade, I was assigned to the Bureau of Ships Computational Project, Harvard University. So there we have it, that was the start of my extremely long relationship with computing. It was 1943.

My boss was Howard Aiken, who was a bully and a genius, and I respected him. The day I joined he greeting me with "Where the **** have you been? Here, compute the coefficients of these arc tangent series by next Thursday!" He pointed me at the electromechanical Harvard Mark I machine, and just left me to it. Let me tell you about Aiken, and how he thought that our ghosts Charles Babbage and Ada Lovelace were "personally addressing him from the past." Aiken had written a superb thesis around 1937 that he called the *Proposed Automatic Calculating Machine*, where he discussed Babbage's machines of 120 years before, and how they had evolved from punch-card programming to electromagnetic desk calculators. But he reckoned that Lovelace's theories had hardly been evolved at all.

He said that computer calculations were incredibly time consuming and clunky, but in fact there was no need for humans to be involved at all. He built on the foundations of Lovelace's work to explain that computers could automate simple arithmetic, sequence control, values, memory, storage, responses and printed records, and not just for numbers but for symbols as well. In other words it took more than a century for this self-opinionated male to catch on to the ideas of a female genius. But unlike Lovelace and Babbage, Howard Aiken was determined not to be stymied by any lack of funds. He went to IBM with an eye on tempting

Uncle Sam and got talking about the wider use of his proposed computer for radio comms, theoretical physics, sociology, astronomy and of course the military.

I don't want you to get bored by jargon, but bear with me as I set out the four areas we were working on to replace the sort of punch card machines which were then manufactured by corporations like IBM. First, the existing accounting machines were designed to handle positive numbers, whereas our machine would deal with negatives as well. Second, our machine would handle changes in functions as well as predicting the probabilities of these changes. Third, we would fully automate all the calculations. And fourth, we would design our machine so that it could handle lines of code, not just columns. The clincher was that we declared such a machine would handle the relationships between one eight-significant-figure and another eight-significant-figure in less than five seconds. Work on the *Harvard Mark 1* started in May 1939, I joined the team December 1943, then nine months and $200,000 later, IBM formally presented the operational *Mark 1* to Harvard.

Alright, alright, here comes the famous story about the machine breaking down and me finding a dead moth inside with its wings gumming up the works. That's true enough, but I categorically did NOT coin the word "bug" to describe a computer glitch. That expression had been in use since 1878 when Edison coined it in a letter to William Orton the President of the Western Union telephone company. The word that I gave the English language was not bug, it was "debugging." Got it? Good, let's move on.

As soon as I learned how to program the *Harvard Mark 1*, I set about putting together its *Manual of Operations*. It was eventually published in 1946 as a 500-page book where I outlined all the basic operating principles not just of the Harvard computer, but of all computing machines. That could have been enough to earn me a chapter in this modest little book, but I did so much more to deserve my place here.

In 1952 I went and wrote the world's first compiler. It was for a Sperry-Rand computer called the *A-o System*. I just took all the program routines I'd been using for the past few years and put them on tape, one after the other, each with their own call-up number. Then all the computer had to do was spool through the tape, find them, bring them over and do the math. Why did I do it? At the time I said I did it because I was lazy, but that's not true. I did it because I was impatient, and I wanted the business of computer programming to be handed over to machines so I could return to being a mathematician.

For the hard of thinking, a compiler is just a language, it's an intermediate program that takes instructions typed by a human in the English language and translates those instructions into a machine language that can be understood by the target computer. Got it? Good. Let's move on again.

When my compiler was launched it got treated like garbage, and I was bitterly disappointed. Nobody would use it. I got patronised and fobbed off that computers were not for programs, they were for arithmetic. Besides, computers couldn't read English. Those men were totally allergic to change, and I had one hell of job trying to prove that letters of the alphabet are just another kind of symbol for a computer to recognise and manipulate. But I proved it in the end, and my code became the basis for the COBOL computer language, that's short for COmmon Business-Orientated Language, if you're interested. I developed a version called FLOW-MATIC which I aimed at business to use for payrolls and billing, and it slowly got adopted. By the end of 1956 I had UNIVAC computers understanding over twenty statements in English. It was like getting infants to grasp the concept of letters being a code for sounds then watch the light-bulb moment when they start reading for themselves.

During the War, and after, I was put under a lot of pressure by Howard Aiken, and by the Navy, and by the corporates, and yes, by me. Extreme pressure. The drinking culture was normal, but I couldn't handle it and I became reliant. I admit it, I became an alcoholic. After the War it got worse and worse, and I just tried to keep a lid on it. Then I got arrested for drunk and disorderly in Philly, and thrown in the cells. The secret was out. I tried to kill myself. My preferred method was drowning, which is kind of apt for a Navy officer, I think you'll agree. Got it? Good. Let's move on one final time.

I dried out. I fell off the wagon. I got sober again. I relapsed again. So it goes. But I was a Navy reservist all through my career, until they forced me to retire as Commander in 1966. When I got sober in 1967 they recalled me to active duty and I reenlisted, serving as Director of the Navy Programming Languages Group. That's when I standardised all the Navy's computer languages. In 1973 they promoted me to the rank of Captain, and that's when they started calling me Amazing Grace. I got promoted Commodore in 1983, and finally Rear Admiral in 1985. In August 1986, when I retired from the Navy aged 79, I was the oldest serving officer in the US Armed Forces. So then I went and got myself hired as senior consultant to the Digital Equipment Corporation. Of course I did. I worked at DEC until I dropped.

When they named the Navy's most advanced destroyer the USS Grace Hopper, I guess all those young sailors glued to their missile simulations and video-games didn't even know that it was this wrinkled old crone, the real life Grace Hopper, who had made it all possible for them.

I never let the fact that I was a woman get in the way, either when I was young or old. I suppose I just ignored the way my gender was oppressed in the Navy and in civilian life as well, and never let that limit me. But then I had been doing that since I started out. All I really wanted was for programming to be user-friendly, and I always believed that my work with computer languages would allow anyone to work with intelligent machines and make life better.

After I died on New Year's Day 1992, they planted me in the Arlington National Cemetery with full military honours.

But my soul goes marching on. If you do a search on the new Grace Hopper GH200 Superchip you'll see it's been designed from the ground up for AI to handle terabytes of data and solve the world's most complex problems.

As for gaming, I was never in the slightest bit interested. I may have made computer programming accessible and even simple, but it was never a game. It was deadly serious.

Grace Hopper, 1946
Courtesy of the Library of Congress National Collection
publication usage LC-USZ62-111439

A MANUAL OF OPERATION
FOR THE
AUTOMATIC SEQUENCE CONTROLLED
CALCULATOR

BY

THE STAFF OF THE COMPUTATION LABORATORY

WITH A FOREWORD BY

JAMES BRYANT CONANT

CAMBRIDGE, MASSACHUSETTS
HARVARD UNIVERSITY PRESS
1946

The Manual of Operation, by Grace Hopper, 1946
Harvard University Press, with thanks for fair use permission.

The Eighth Ghost

Josef Kates 1921–2018

The games machine, 1950

G race Hopper was my kinda woman, in that old fashioned way, but my-oh-my, what about that Hedy Lamarr! Hedy and me had something in common and I don't mean just in our inventions. We were both born in Vienna, only seven years apart, and here we are together at last with only Grace Hopper between us. Hedy Lamarr! What a face. What a body. What a gorgeous gal she was. And what a helluva brain she had. Maybe I should have named my games-machine after her, but *Hedy The Brain* doesn't quite have the pizzaz of *Bertie The Brain*. Anyway folks, let me begin at the beginning, at least let me begin at my beginning. Are you ready? OK then, here we go.

I was born as Josef Katz in the spring of 1921, and my folks ran the local grocery store. They had too many children and not enough time for any them, and the four youngest kids including me got packed off to the *Kinderheim*. If I tell you I had a happy childhood, then I'd be lying. My childhood was miserable. I was just another snot-nose Jewish kid growing up in the most depressed and anti-Semitic part of Vienna. My world was horrible and I was very, very lonely. I got attacked all the time. I don't mean verbally attacked, I mean I got my goddam teeth knocked out.

Well, I was just seventeen when Germany invaded my country. I was walking down the street and I heard the trucks coming a long while before I saw them, loaded with Nazis, and there were crowds of *arschlochen* celebrating. My school stayed shut for two weeks, and then the first day I went back I found that I was only one of a handful of Jews who had returned. I knew it was time to quit, not just to quit my school but to quit Austria period.

But so many in our Jewish community were in denial. So many of them thought things would blow over somehow and that they would be alright. When I tried to convince my parents to leave, my father held out because he hoped that our new political masters might actually benefit the family business. But I was the one who was fresh from getting bullied and attacked, and I had not just read the writing on the wall, I'd had my head smacked against it. Me and a friend fled to Italy. We spent our first night as refugees hidden on the deck of one of those gondola things, so I guess we'd gotten to Venice.

My folks were warned to get out of Austria often enough, until they eventually wised up and hid in the same *kinderheim* that I had been banished to, while their home and our corner shop and the synagogue got destroyed around them. But they were luckier than most, and even though my father was jailed simply for being who he was, he bribed his way out and somehow they all got out of Nazi territory the day before the War began. All except my auntie Rosa, she didn't make it.

When I arrived on the boat in England, I was near enough eighteen years old and ready to fight me some Germans, so I enlisted in the British Army. The authorities showed their gratitude by arresting me as an enemy alien and locking me up in an internment camp. It took me two years to get out. So I showed my gratitude in return by agreeing to be sent to Canada, where I was rearrested and flung into a series of camps for German prisoners of war and enemies of the state. When the Kraut prisoners discovered I was Jewish, they beat the *drek* out of me all over again. But hey, at least I was alive, and eventually my luck turned.

In one camp I was given work as a lumberjack, and then I was taught how to use a machine for making fishing nets. That machine was a descendant of an automated process designed by the first ghost in this book, Joseph Jacquard, and I guess that's where my real education began.

The Governor spotted my interest and gave me the chance to study. I leapt at the chance, even if I had to use toilet paper for my notebooks. Which I did. It was not as if the Canadian students were dumb, it was that some of us refugees had the burning desire to make good and achieve something special. We took our exams through a scheme organised by McGill University in Montreal, and I came out on top. That was not top in the whole of Montreal, that was top in the whole province. The guy who came second was Walter Kohn, my fellow prisoner from Austria. One day he would win the Nobel Prize for chemistry.

Before the end of the War, I got recognised as a victim of Nazi aggression. I got released, I moved to Toronto, I got married, we had four kids, I idolised them, my wife died just before our Golden Wedding, I was an old man but I got married again soon after. When my second wife died, I was a very old man and I used internet dating to look for my very own Hedy Lamarr. But I guess you don't care about any of that, because what you really care about is how I invented the world's first arcade games machine. Am I right? Sure I am. OK then, here we go again.

I got my first proper job at the Imperial Optical Company in Toronto, and they put me in charge of all the precision optics for the Royal Canadian Navy. Then I went to work for the Rogers Vacuum Tube Company and developed radio tubes and vacuum tubes. Then I walked into the University of Toronto, and walked out with Honours in physics and math, a Masters in applied math and a Doctorate in physics. And while I was there I helped design and build UTEC, the first computer in the whole of Canada. I was leading the team alongside a real *mensch*, an electrical engineer called Alfred Ratz, and our UTEC soon got named the Man-Made Brain.

It was pay-back time for Rogers, as far as I was concerned, and my job was to design the memory and control system, and back then those early computers needed ten or more radio vacuum tubes just to handle the simplest binary addition. My artificial brain was way too big, way too expensive and way too clunky. I spent too many days trying to solve the problem, and then I spent too many nights as well. I was lying awake in the early hours thinking about how to solve these problems when I had a notion. What if I could design a single tube that would do the work of multiple tubes and cut out a load of the circuitry and network connections. And that's exactly what I did.

I designed a completely new tube that wouldn't replace a standard electronic vacuum tube but instead it would fit inside. My new internal tube would tote up a load of ones and zeros, and then carry-over a zero or a one as necessary. In other words, it would calculate binary numbers. I called it my Additron Tube. But I never intended to create the world's first arcade game. No sir.

All I wanted was to do, and all the sales boys wanted from me, was to demonstrate what we thought was a big technical advance, and to demonstrate it in a way folks could understand. I reckoned that other computer nuts would understand what was going on, but the public needed something simple. And what could be more simple than a kid's game. And what kid's game is more simple than what I call *Nullen und Kreuzen*, what the Canadians call Tic-Tac-Toe, or what the Brits call Noughts-And-Crosses.

Tic-Tac-Toe was kinda the perfect game because it was easy to play, it was quick to play and everyone already knew how to play it, so the public could take on the challenge of playing against a machine and try and beat it. As far as the programming was concerned, the player had a real small number of options to choose from, so the machine's decisions were very simple and I could make the responses instant. More than that, I could build in levels of difficulty and delays to make the gameplay more exciting.

If the programming was pretty straightforward, then the presentation was even simpler. Back in 1950, sci-fi movies were all the rage with titles like *King Of The Rocket Men, The Day The Earth Stood Still* and *Spaceship One.* Isaac Asimov's *I Robot* was released, and the comic books were stiff with mad scientists and their electronic brains. So I came up with the name Bertie The Brain, and housed him in a whiz-bang magic robot cabinet twice as tall as a human.

I didn't have any fancy screen, and Bertie's head was just a three-by-three square grid, with lightbulbs that lit up each square with an X or an O depending on the gameplay. The display was big enough for a crowd to stand around and watch as a game progressed, without the need to get too close to the action. There was a smaller 9-square input pad at *schlong* height, where the human player would command their moves, and I added a primitive electronic score-board at eye-level that showed a running total of games won by the "electronic brain" versus the "human brain". There were also three advert boards for the Rogers Majestic lab where Bertie was built, which was the whole point of the enterprise.

When a human pressed a square on the input pad, it sent a command to my Additron tubes in Bertie's guts to calculate the binary notation and decide what Bertie's response would be. In fact, Bertie couldn't lose, and the best a human challenger could ever hope for was a draw, so I added a routine to deliberately make Bertie's intelligence *fakakta* if necessary. I thought it would be great if now and then there was a chance of a kid beating him at the game.

Bertie made his debut in the summer of 1950 at the Canadian National Exhibition in Toronto, where inventions had been on show since the first expo there a century before. We placed him in the middle of all the latest models of radios, TVs and other gadgets on the Rogers stand, then when the doors opened we waited to see if there was any interest. And was there! Bertie was a sensation! Nobody had ever seen anything like it outside of sci-fi, let alone get the chance to pit their wits against it. Folks started queueing up to play and see if they could beat my creation, and even more folks just stood around watching the action to cheer things on. I guess I didn't just go and invent the video arcade game, I invented stadium esports and celebrity endorsements. Let me tell you what happened.

At the time the most popular kids entertainer in the world was a guy called Danny Kaye, even the British princesses Elizabeth and Margaret were fans of his. Danny was passing through Toronto and somehow we got him to show up on the stand to go head-to-head with Bertie, and we just happened to invite the press along at the same time. Danny Kaye tried and tried to beat Bertie at tic-tac-toe but he just couldn't do it. The cameras and the crowd loved it, which is more than can be said for Danny, and even though he kept on acting the clown I could see he was doing it through gritted teeth. The more the illuminated sign lit up with 'Computer Brain Wins', the less he liked it. So I did the only thing I could do, and threw the switch to lower the difficulty to infant level. When Danny Kaye finally beat the first arcade game in the world he went and did a dance of joy in front of the crowd, history was made and that's what the cameras captured.

Bertie never malfunctioned once and he performed faultlessly the whole time the exhibition ran. My Additron tube had proved itself a winner. Then the whole damn thing got dismantled and became obsolete and then got forgotten. I may have reduced a computer's size by a factor of ten, but it didn't take long for solid-state devices to beef things up by a factor of a million to one. As for me, I just didn't realise the significance of what I'd done. If the transistor revolution had started ten years later I would have been *zeyer reykh*, but hey, who wants to be a billionaire. I had a great life, and I had a long one, and now I'm not just the ghost in my machine, I'm the ghost in every arcade machine since. I'm in all those cabinets with flashing lights and hot buttons all over the planet. I was in every *Space Invader* and *Pong* and *PacMan* and I'm still in every console and handheld and esports arena.

Just remember me as a nice guy. A nice guy with a funny European accent who got his name changed from Katz to Kates. A *Hebe* who liked a bacon sandwich and gave the world a whole lot of fun. Abyssinia.

Josef Kates aged 92
Photo by Vince Talotta, with kind permission The Toronto Star,
courtesy of Toronto Public Library.

Bertie the Brain, 1950

The Ninth Ghost

Willy Higinbotham 1910-1994

The Smart Videogame, 1958

here are heroes and villains in all good fairy tales and
all bad adventure games. They are made that way so
everyone can cheer the hero and boo the villain. For
me the greatest hero in this book is Ghost number Five, Paul
Otlet. He is my inspiration as a hero who wanted to harness
technology for peace. And I, my friends, am the man who
helped develop the atomic bomb, so you may think I am a
gosh-darned hypocritical villain. Well, I intend to prove to
you that I am not. And on the way, I'll tell you why I created
the world's first smart videogame ever.

Come closer. Are you sitting comfortably? Then I'll
begin.

Once upon a time, long long ago and far far away, in a
little town called Bridgeport in the little state of Connecticut,
there lived an Irish Presbyterian pastor called Robert
Higinbotham. In January 1910, the Reverend Robert married

his sweetheart Dorothea Schauffler, who was a fine lady from a German family of teachers and musicians, and by a miracle of timing it was exactly nine months later that I, William Alfred, was born into this world, the first of their six children.

The Higinbothams moved to the little town of Caledonia in New York state when I was just seven years old, and before another seven years had passed I had begun my interest in gadgets and science, messing around with radio kits and trying to tune in to those very first commercial radio stations. Luckily the cellphone had yet to be invented so at least I saw daylight now and again. Unfortunately, cigarettes had been invented, and I was an early adopter.

The town only had a population of around two thousand souls, but we had a high school and that high school had two things that I liked a whole lot. The first thing I liked a whole lot was a tennis court and the second thing I liked a whole lot was a kindly man who taught me his favourite subject, which was physics. I took to physics like a duck to water. But my duck pond wasn't big enough for further education, and I migrated 270 miles east to Williams College, Massachusetts, for my undergraduate degree in physics, then I migrated 200 miles west again to Cornell University as a graduate. One day, all the duckponds in the land, big and small, grew cloudy and afraid because World War II had begun.

All the clever ducks, the ones with expertise in science, were sent to help their country's cause in some way, and this clever duck was invited to help with the research at the Massachusetts Institute of Technology Radiation Laboratory, and from 1941 to 1943 I spread my wings with a new form of defense technology that they called radar.

It turned out that I was a very clever duck indeed, and I found myself swimming in a top-secret duckpond at the Los Alamos National Laboratory, heading up their electronics department. The project we were working on brought together some of the greatest scientific ducks of the day, with famous names like Oppenheimer, Heisenberg, von Neumann and Bush, as well as migrating ducks like Teller, Franck and Einstein. We were building the atomic bomb. It was my team that developed the electronics for the world's first nuclear explosion, as well as all its measuring instruments, and I personally created the radar display for the B28 bomber. But please don't be afraid and please read on.

I had a baby sister duckling, and four kid brother ducklings. Dorothy and John did ok, but my brothers Phil and Fred both got killed young in the war. It was their deaths and the understanding of the horror of nuclear weapons that affected my future big time. I decided to fly away from the secret duckpond and move to a special zoo to help found the Federation of American Scientists nuclear nonproliferation organisation. In fact I was its first chairman. But did all the animals in the zoo listen? Well, some did, and there again, some didn't.

The zoo was called the Brookhaven National Laboratory, on Long Island, and I became head zookeeper of the Instrumentation Division. Once every year we opened our doors for Visitors Days, and every single year I got exasperated with the exhibits that demonstrated our achievements in the most boring way it was possible to imagine. Nine years to be precise. Our computers were what you might call cutting edge, but they just sat there and glowered, and it wasn't until October 1958 that I realised I'd had enough and couldn't take it any more. I knew I had to liven the place up.

Then I remembered the high school where it all began for me, and I remembered that tennis court. What if I could create a game for visitors to the National Lab that would not only show what we could do, but also show it had a relevance to society, and above all turn it all into a whole lot of fun.

I only had two weeks before the gates of the zoo would be thrown open, and I got two of my keepers to help, Dave Potter and Bob Dvorak. We worked out a routine to alternate a computer output and make it perform weird acts on command, then it took me no more than four hours to rough out a game design. If I remember rightly it was an analog computer, a Systron-Donner Model 30. We got everything debugged (thanks for the terminology, Grace) and running in another ten days, which is when I called my creation *Tennis For Two*.

The action took place on the circular screen of an oscilloscope. An oscilloscope is a magic instrument that displays electrical signals to show how they change over a short interval of time, and I used it at the lab to test and debug my circuit designs. The oscilloscope model I used had a 5-inch diameter DuMont cathode-ray screen to show its results. We rigged a pair of hand-held controllers so that two people could play a simulated game of tennis, and *Tennis for Two* went down in history as the first interactive video game. I made it react to each player's decisions and I also programmed it to display motion.

We opened the zoo to the public at 10am on Saturday 18 October 1958 and it caused a feeding frenzy. A very happy one. People stood in line in their hundreds to play.

The tennis court was a sideways view shown on my oscilloscope screen. The ball was a moving dot, very bright and very sci-fi, and it bounced towards alternate sides of the net leaving ghostly trails behind it. The players could serve and volley using buttons and rotating dials on their controllers, and they had control over the angle of swing and the power of the shot. OK, so the tennis racquets were invisible, but hey that's showbiz for you.

Tennis for Two was a big hit, and the following year it grabbed the headlines again as our key exhibit. For the 1959 version I added gravity control, so players could simulate a game of tennis on the Moon or on Jupiter. It wasn't until later that I realised my electronic tennis court looked like a duckpond. Anyway, I lost interest in video games after that, because my work against the spread of nuclear weapons was much more important.

I never took out a patent on the game. Besides, even if I had gone down the patent pathway the game rights would have belonged to the government. The instruction manual that came with the computer contained all the ideas anyway, like how to produce bouncing shapes, how to leave trails and how to plot trajectories. So what was there for me to patent? Did the guy who ripped off my game and made *Pong* have a patent? I don't really know and I don't really care. Beyond the duckpond and the zoo I did take out more than twenty other patents though, but I'd rather be remembered for my work in the cause of nuclear nonproliferation. It was because of that the Federation of American Scientists named their headquarters Higinbotham Hall when I died in 1994. That was a real honour.

Before I leave you, I'd like to thank my parents for having me, my three wives for marrying me, our kids and their kids for putting up with me, and you readers for allowing me to tell you my story.

And if you're interested, it was Emphysema the Cigarette Dragon that got me in the end. But I made it to 84, and that's no fairy story.

Willy Higinbotham, 1958
photo by H. Davis, AIP open access
use of image ref# nbla:287931

Tennis For Two, 1958
on DuMont Lab Oscilloscope 304-A
Brookhaven National Laboratory, Public Domain

The Tenth Ghost

Lou Ottens 1926-2021

The Cassette, 1963

I have no doubt that there is one invention that kickstarted gaming as you know it today. It happened before esports, before social media, before online gaming, before consoles, before cartridges and micros, way before any of that. And that one invention was of a device that came to be called the compact cassette. It was nothing more than a few yards of eighth-inch magnetic tape spooled inside a little plastic case that could fit in the palm of your hand. It was four inches wide, by two and a half inches deep, by half an inch thick. It was cheap, it was simple and it was the perfect way to store and play computer data for the most basic of home systems. And that's not all, the compact cassette simultaneously gave birth to the biggest illegal industry in the history of entertainment - software piracy.

I am the ghost of that invention, because I am the man who created it. And the funny thing is, I don't believe in ghosts! My name was Lodewijk Frederik Ottens, and you are more than welcome to call me Lou. I was a Dutchman, from a little village called Bellingwolde, where my parents were the schoolteachers. Bellingwolde is right on the border with Germany, so I had a ringside seat when our German neighbours invaded my country in 1940. I was a tinkerer of valves and circuits. I was always inventing gadgets and devices, and I had already built my own radio set to listen to broadcasts on the BBC, but of course the Nazis wanted to dominate the airwaves and they would jam any unauthorised frequencies. So I built myself a directional antenna to bypass their jammers. I called it my *Germannen-Krautfilter*, and I remember me and my family gathering round to listen to our Queen Wilhelmina speaking to us on free Radio Oranje. She was a clever old thing, a real survivor, the world's first woman billionaire, and she spoke to us from exile over the water in England. As for me, I was a fourteen year old whizkid.

When the war was over I went and studied mechanical engineering in the city of Delft, where I paid my way by moonlighting as a drafting technician, until I graduated in 1952 after a lot of hard work and a little bit of luck. There was only one real opportunity for a youngster with my skills, and that was with the mighty Philips company, recovering in a post-war world, and back in business once again to produce radios, televisions and record players. But the important thing as far as this story is concerned is that they were also experimenting with tape-recorders for the home market. So I went and applied and I got accepted, and Philips became my first legitimate employer. It's not that I am very boring, it's more like they were the perfect fit for me, because I stayed with Philips until the day I retired. And yes, in case you haven't guessed it, I ended up running the company. Of course I did.

Like most of the newcomers at Philips, I began my career in their main complex in the Dutch town of Eindhoven, where the company had been founded way back in 1891. I plodded away for five years in the mechanisation department, which is when I met my Margo and we married. But my work there wasn't very exciting, so when Philips opened a brand new audio factory just over the Belgian border in Hasselt, I jumped at the chance of moving on. It took me three years to become head of new product development there, and I was ready to ride the growing wave of consumerism in home entertainment.

I thought that creating new turntables and loudspeakers was all very well, but I believed that there was a major gap in the market for a portable tape-recorder, so I set up a development team to start from the basics in terms of design, simplicity and cost. The result was my EL3585 portable tape-recorder project, and to cut a long story short it went and sold over a million units.

So there I was. I had become the Philips Golden Boy, and I used my new-found kudos to push ahead with plans for a more ambitious innovation. Everyone had a transistor radio by then, and a lot of those little radios were small enough to carry in your pocket. What I thought the world needed was not only a portable tape-recorder, but one that was user-controlled, extremely cheap, had a reasonable sound quality and that you could also fit in your pocket. And I thought that it was important for such a product to deliver hours of entertainment without having to change the batteries all the time. Between me and you, I was never completely convinced about what they said about my abilities or talent, and for much of the time I just busked it, riding the successes and burying the mistakes.

At the time, all tape-recorders worked on the same reel-to-reel principle where a spool of tape was used to record and play audio signals by pulling it past a magnetic head, using spindles and rubber wheels and regulators to get a constant speed. One night I wanted to play some classical music that I had recorded off the radio on my home reel-to-reel, and I was a bit clumsy. The tape twisted, then it jammed, then it unspooled all over the place, and I got really annoyed, especially because the machine was a model that my team had designed. I knew in my heart that it was a bit unoriginal and clunky and if I had really put my mind to it then I would have started from scratch with a completely new method of playing the tape. So I gave up trying to untwist all the tape and went to sleep on the problem. Next morning as soon as I woke up I did a few sketches and calculations, then I went into work with my ideas set out on paper and carried in my briefcase.

Basically, I needed a tape that was protected inside a self-enclosed plastic case, and I thought I could use the existing RCA tape cartridge, and build a portable tape recorder round it. The RCA had been around since 1958, and it coincided with the launch of vinyl stereo records. It was convenient, and it gave home users thirty minutes play time each side. But the problem was it was too damn big, seven inches by five, so any player would end up being almost as big as the reel-to-reel portable we had already produced. It also ran way too fast for what I had in mind. So I went right back to basics.

I took a block of wood and cut it back and cut it back until it could fit inside my jacket pocket. If I was going to produce a pocket recorder then that's where I needed to start. And if my block of wood was to determine the size of the machine, then I would need a compact tape cassette to fit inside it. Years later the Philips Museum wanted to put my little block of wood on display, and I had to confess that I lost it after using it to prop up my car jack for changing a flat tyre. I know I could have faked another one for the museum, but that wasn't my style.

I brought a design team of a dozen workers together, all experienced and hands-on, and I could use experts from the Eindhoven factory as well as at Hasselt when I needed them. Remember, the project was all about size, and the marketing boys wanted to be able to say it would be "smaller than a pack of cigarettes", which I don't suppose would go down too well with the anti-smokers these days. We didn't care a lot about the sound quality to begin with, in fact I thought a pocket recorder would be used mostly for speech, you know, by journalists and for office memos. As it turned out, even with the first working prototype the sound was way better than I had expected. The prototype model was codenamed the EL330, and we increased the playing time up to sixty minutes a side, so it could beat the RCA cartridge.

We launched the compact cassette recorder at the 1963 Berlin Radio Show, and it was met with what I can only call amused indifference. It didn't spark much interest at all in the audio world, but there was this bunch of Japanese in their black suits at the show who photographed it in great detail. They were sneaky about it, but I spotted them. And that's when I made a breakthrough decision. I knew my design would be copied and that cheaper knock-off models would appear, and somehow I managed to persuade the Philips executives to offer the designs and patents to rival manufacturers for free.

The Sony corporation nearly bit our hand off, and National Panasonic followed, and then everyone piled in. I expected my compact cassette to be a success, but not a revolution. As it turned out, I had created the new global standard. A cassette released in one country would work just the same in any other country. By the time I died, more than a hundred billion compact cassettes had been sold all over the world. And as for the Sony Walkman, heaven knows how many that sold, in fact I think it's still going.

In the 1960s everyone began to make their own mixtapes, then it exploded with the DJs and underground music, and the punk bands and hip-hop. Soon the record companies were releasing albums on my compact cassettes simultaneously with vinyl. Cassette players became standard equipment in cars all over the world, and the same for telephone answering machines. In the 1970s, a brand new market in audiobooks on cassette started up. And there were things that I never anticipated at all, like my cassettes becoming catalysts for social change because of their small size and toughness, and because they were cheap, easy to copy and easy to hide. There was no internet then, no text messaging or social media, and it was compact cassettes that helped spread underground culture behind the Iron Curtain, and they were used to challenge the ruling regimes in nations like Egypt, Iran, Chile, Afghanistan, you name it.

I grew the number of employees to over five thousand at our Hasselt centre before I was appointed Technical Director of Philips Audio. And that's where I moved on to my next media revolution, which was the compact disc. Yes, that was me too.

It was after I launched the CD in 1979 that something happened to really surprise me, and that something was how my compact cassette affected computer gaming. At Philips we had bought the American Magnavox games company and our own Videopac console was competing well against the Atari 2600. Then not only in my country but all across Europe the kids started playing home video-games on imported micro machines like the ZX Spectrum and Commodore 64. Almost all the software was produced in the UK by enthusiasts and bedroom companies, and it was loaded into the micros via compact cassettes, sometimes with professional inlays, sometimes just with photocopied instructions.

It took gamers about five minutes to work out that they could get their gaming software for free, simply by duplicating copies of the cassettes tape-to-tape. I remember that Amstrad even brought out a dedicated twin-cassette machine to do just that. Then the organised pirates moved in, using high-speed multi duplicators that were capable of making hundreds of pirate copies an hour from a legit original. I had created a monster. For every legitimate copy of a computer game there seemed to be a dozen pirate copies. And as it turned out, I slew my own monster when I developed the compact disc. It was a better product than the cassette, so it was time to move on.

I don't believe in eternity. I don't believe in ghosts. I died when I was 94 years old, and when your time has gone, it's time to disappear. Thank you and goodbye.

Lou Ottens, 2007
Jordi Huisman, Nederlands Koninkliijk Institut van Ingenieurs
with permission from Creative Care International
License #20190314100089525

Atari 410 Cassette Program Recorder, 1979
Mel Croucher, private archive

The Eleventh Ghost

Mabel Addis 1912-2004

The Strategy Game, 1964

S ome time around 1969, by way of my daughter
Alexandra's twenty-fifth birthday celebration, we went
out together to see Stanley Kubrick's sci-fi blockbuster
2001: A Space Odyssey. I remember there was a great intro
sequence, where a bunch of ape-men encounter an extra-
terrestrial monolith, which has the power to inspire the boss
ape with the notion of toolmaking. The boss ape throws a
thigh bone into the air in an ecstasy of realisation, and the
camera tracks that prehistoric bone until it morphs into a
huge spaceship, all to illustrate how humanity has evolved
from ape-man to modern man. My point is that if Josef
Kates' *Bertie The Brain* represents that bone, then my
Sumerian Game represents that spaceship. And in my case the
evolution only took fourteen years from *Bertie* to my game.
So this chapter is all about what I created, which is reckoned
to be the first computer game to introduce storylines,
characters, scenes, levels, role-playing, civilisation-building,

trading, edutainment, non-linear narratives, audio-visuals, in fact the whole darned shooting match. Are you ready? Here we go.

I was born Mabel Lorene Holmes in the Spring of 1912 in Mount Vernon. Don't let the bucolic name fool you, Mount Vernon is just North of The Bronx in New York City, where my Pa Jimmy Holmes ran a building supply outfit. When I was young I always dreamed of digging up the past and becoming an archeologist, but my Ma vetoed anything like that. Perhaps she didn't have a lot of imagination, after all her name was Mabel and that's the name she gave me. Anyhow, I did the next best thing, and as soon as I graduated high school I was off to study ancient history at Barnard in Manhattan and ended up with a Master's in education from Columbia. Then I became a teacher, which could have been the end of my ghost-in-the-machine story for you. But it wasn't.

I taught for half a century, starting in a one-room schoolhouse and ending up in an elementary school in Katonah, Westchester, population one thousand. I could tell you about my two marriages, my wonderful daughter, my history research and my travels to visit classical antiquities, but I won't. As a matter of fact I can't, because I can't remember very much at all. I got Alzheimer's disease in the end, but anyway I made it to the age of 92. Besides, I'm not supposed to say that I'm needing help writing my story for you. I do see the humour in that though, a ghost in need of a ghost writer.

To continue, there I was teaching fourth-grade when what they called "a crisis in small-school-district education" came along. We had gotten ourselves overextended, which is a polite way of saying we couldn't keep up with the modernised curriculum and our school was failing, even though the kids said they loved my classes, especially when I brought history alive for them. The Westchester County Board of education got called in and things were looking bleak at my school, that is until the superintendent of the

Board, Mr. Gividen, visited the mid-county office of IBM and reckoned their new-fangled computers could be used as a teaching aid. That was in 1962.

The following year Mr. Gividen went and invited teachers in our district to see if there was some way of bringing computerised simulations into the classroom, to broaden the minds of our young students. It was a unique opportunity of course, though I didn't realise that until a while after.

Most of the other teachers just went and reinvented the wheel, mapping out ideas for games like tic-tac-toe and checkers. There had been an IBM mainframe running an automated chess engine since 1957, and that monster took around eight minutes to make each move. And things had not gotten a lot faster by '62, but over at Dartmouth a youngster called Slug Russel came up with *Space War*, using a cathode ray tube to simulate a fight between two teensy-weensy spaceships. I didn't criticise my fellow-teacher's efforts at the time, but between you and me I thought they were crappy. Can I say crappy now I'm dead? I thought they were crappy little sideshows to what a computer was capable of bringing to the classroom.

A computer can take input and generate output and a century before I got the message, Ada Lovelace realised that a computer can handle abstract concepts like symbols, sounds and logic. And a computer can recognise strings of numbers representing text and then act accordingly. That was my starting point for the notion that interacting with a computer could actually generate emotion. And because nobody had written the rule book on how to create an educational and emotional computer game, I wrote it myself.

They say you should always write about what you know best, and what I knew best was ancient history. Not blood-soaked battles or derring-do, but how people actually lived, and as well as a computer program I used a slide protector and a tape recorder to help set my scenes. Nobody gave me credit at the time, but I had gone and invented multi-media entertainment along with what a couple of decades later the world would call Strategy Games.

I was championed by Bruce Moncreiff over at IBM's theoretical research unit, and he proposed that I should exploit my knowledge of history to try and teach the kids economic theory. That's where *The Sumerian Game* was hatched. I designed it and wrote it from top to bottom, and Bruce got his colleague Billy McKay to tame the IBM and help program it. Billy wrote it in the Fortran programming language, it was text only and it took two whole years for him to complete the task. As I told you, the accompanying images were simply projected onto the classroom wall, and the audio was played through the school tape recorder. According to modern historians, I was the first video-game writer ever, and I'm not going to argue.

So here's the outline, and I'll keep it simple. I wanted to teach my my sixth graders the basics of economic theory, so I put them in charge of an ancient Mesopotamian city, in Sumer, around 3,500 BC. I kept the gameplay to three levels. In Level-1 you just went around making tools and growing crops. In Level-2 I made things more complicated as the economy diversified. And in Level-3 you traded and interacted with other city-states. But I made it all personal, in fact I made the gameplay first person. The player took the role of Luduga the royal ruler, but the player's decisions were all based on text prompts from the royal steward Urbaba.

So there you have it. I had gone and invented immersive, narrative-based video-gaming and created multiple storylines where the outcome depended on the actions of the player. This was eight years before that dumb game *Pong* was hailed as the first proper video-game. And let me tell you you my *Sumerian Game* was seven years before the first popular role-playing-game *Oregon Trail* where the player struggles to survive a Wild West journey in their wagon-train and which mimicked my gameplay mercilessly. Ah well, they say imitation is the sincerest form of flattery, so I should have been extremely flattered by that.

After my slides and audio set each scene, the player
entered their commands using an IBM 1050 teleprinter,
which looked like a golfball typewriter and which was linked
to an IBM 7090 mainframe. As for the player themself, they
had no idea what was coming, and I made sure the gameplay
threw in plenty of surprises.

"Luduga, I fear that the people have angered our god,
Ningrisa. He alone could have sent that fire across the fields
to destroy half your crops. This is a very serious loss. I trust
that you can cover it from your inventory." My students soon
got hooked. They really seemed to care about the effect their
gaming had on these fantasy people. Their decisions affected
everything from social structures to harvests, by way of
supply, demand and taxes. If they got it wrong they felt
responsible for killing off the population. If they got it right,
their imaginary society prospered and grew. Not to mention
the floods, parasites, rot, plague and wildfires. And at the
end of each Level, the computer would generate a full report
to the Ruler - the player - to give the status of their
population, their assets and their sovereignty.

That wasn't the end of it by a long way. I didn't rest on
my laurels, and the main reason for that was because I
wasn't awarded any laurels to rest on. They came after I died.
I was given a job to do, and I did it, no more, no less. After
two years of feedback and print-outs from my students, I
started work on Phase Two of *The Sumerian Game*. I was one
of three teachers, each producing our own educational game.
A detailed report covered the results, and involved twenty-
six young students as model players. It was snappily titled
'The Production and Evaluation of Three Computer-Based
Economics Games for the Sixth Grade, by the US Department
of Health, Education and Welfare.'

After I pinpointed exactly how and where my students
got engaged and when and where they lost interest, I was
able to do a major rewrite of my scripts to get rid of irritating
repetitions and fine-tune more dramatic pathways. I guess
you call that play-testing today, back then I called it

empirical education. It was during the rewrite that I added a lot more pre-recorded audio and projected graphics. Here's a quote from the report that summarised it all.

"Mrs. Addis made an amplification and clarification of the objectives, facts, generalizations and concepts implied in the scripts of the three Rulers in the game. The next step was a revision of the parameters with a view to making them more realistic."

And then guess what? They went and cut all funds to the project, and it was abandoned. I wasn't in the slightest bit surprised. Westchester County had gotten a grant of way over a million dollars in today's money for the joint project between the Education Department and IBM, codenamed Project 21948. As for my reward, I had gotten my teacher's pay for my contribution, and that, dear reader, was that.

The Board retained the copyright, there was a glowing write-up in *Time* magazine and soon afterwards another one appeared in *Life* that included the lines, "The kids love being king and become genuinely involved. When the machine relentlessly types out the deaths resulting from an insufficient ration of food, they have been known to pound the keyboards and cry aloud, 'No! Don't let it happen! Please don't let it happen!'"

In 1968 an employee of the Digital Equipment Corporation was giving a talk about computers in education when one of my ex-students got up and said she had played *The Sumerian Game*, then described it in detail. The lecturer's name was Doug Dyment, and he went off and cloned it for his company's new minicomputer. He called it *King of Sumeria*, and later on it morphed into *The Sumer Game*. Then it appeared in the 1971 best-seller *BASIC Computer Games*, and spawned legions of successes including *Hamurabi*, *The Pollution Game*, *Kingdom*, *Santa Paravia*, *Dukedom*, and of course the good ol' *Oregon Trail*.

Me? I went back to my classroom and stayed there until I retired in 1976. My retirement lasted twenty-eight years. Then about ten years after I died I got a posthumous Pioneer

Award for "game updates, in-game narrative experiences, and early iterations of what would become known as cutscenes. Mabel Addis helped pave the way for game elements that wouldn't become mainstream for decades."

I'd like to thank my ghost-writer for repairing my memory, and to you the modern gamer for remembering me. Play well and learn well. Thank you.

Mabel Addis and pupils play The Sumerian Game, 1965
with kind permission from Video Game History Foundation 501(C)3

START

Compute random number, R

Generate no disaster ←———no———— Is R < $\frac{5}{16}$?

Exit to next procedure

yes

Compute another random number, R

Is R < $\frac{9}{16}$? ——yes————————————▷ Reduce harvest 10%

no

Reduce harvest 20% ←——yes—— Is R < $\frac{13}{16}$?

no

Is R < $\frac{15}{16}$? ——yes————▷ Reduce harvest 30%

no

Reduce harvest 40%

———————————▷ Compute another random number, R ◁———————————

Print "Locusts" disaster message ◁——yes—— Is R < $\frac{13}{32}$?

no

Is R < $\frac{26}{32}$? ——yes———▷ Print "God's wrath" disaster message

no

Print "Flood" disaster message

Exit to next procedure

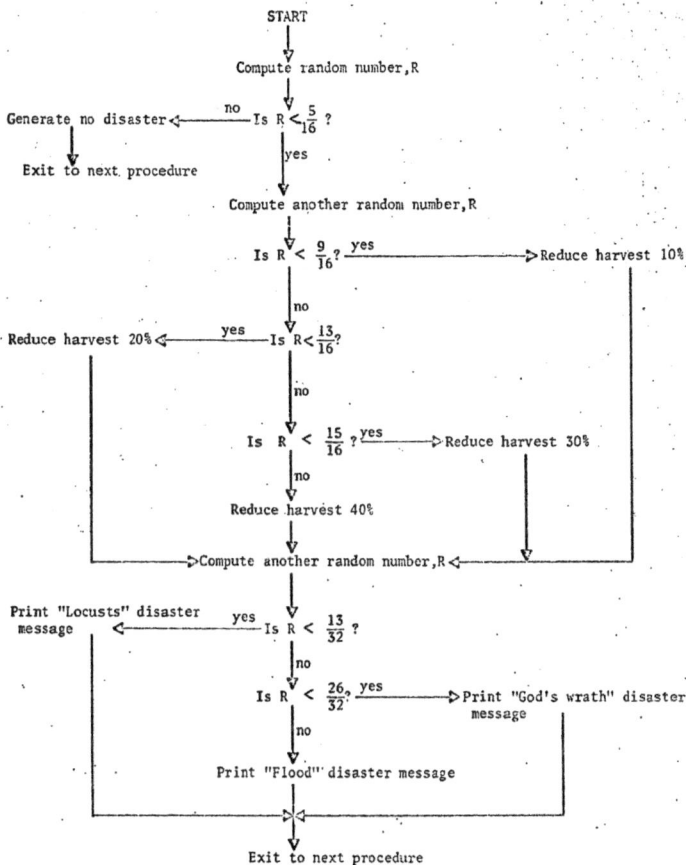

FIGURE 4. NATURAL DISASTER GENERATION PROCEDURE

Sumerian Game, Natural Disaster Generation Procedure
Sumerian Game collection 1962-1967, with kind permission from
Brian Sutton-Smith Library and Archives of Play at The Strong.

The Twelfth Ghost

Ralph Baer 1922-2014

The Games Console, 1972

Yeah, yeah, I know. Here comes another ghost of some Jewish kid who fled Nazi Germany, landed in America and became an electronics engineer. Maybe Hitler deserves his own chapter for changing the history of gaming. On second thoughts, maybe not. I'll cut my own history short for you.

Rudolf Heinrich Baer (that's me) was born in 1922, and flung out of school twelve years later by the anti-Semite laws. So I was self taught, yada yada. My family escaped to New York City and as a juvenile immigrant I was free to make my own future. I got some crummy work in some crummy factory for twelve dollars a week until I saw a flyer at the bus station for volunteers to train as radio service technicians. I quit my job next day and dived into electronics at the National Radio Institute. Then in 1943 I got drafted into the US Army by Uncle Sam and served one year stateside and two years in the London HQ for US military intelligence. That's right folks, they thought I was intelligent, but really I was trained by the best.

I was lucky, the G.I. Bill came in and that gave war veterans like me all kinds of help to adjust to civilian life. I mean, with grants and loans and training. War veterans? Ha! I was still a greenhorn, wet behind the ears, and I never saw any action at all. But I was grateful to my new country for paying my way through the Chicago Institute of Technology.

In 1949 I walked out with a Bachelor of Science degree in television engineering and walked right in to a job at a small outfit called Wappler, making gear that used low frequency pulses. That was kind of bizarre, and I left after a year or so to work for Loral back in New York where I designed signal equipment contracted from IBM. That's where televisions came in to the picture.

I was only a raw graduate, but I had my own ideas, and I proposed to the bosses at my company that we could build games into our brand of TVs to make them more attractive than our competitors. They told me I was an idiot, so I quit. By 1955 I had a job at Sanders Associates, working on military projects again, and the following year I was offered the job of chief engineer.

Are you interested about me marrying Dena, and the arrival of our kids James, Mark and Nancy? I didn't think you were. But I guess you are interested in the fact that I set up a lab in the basement in our home so I could work on my own projects, because I hadn't forgotten about my idea to embed games into TV sets, and that's where this gaming story kicks off again.

Sanders was based in Nashua, a real nice place close to Boston, and I ended up overseeing more than five hundred guys developing electronic systems. I remember exactly where I was when I dug up and revived my notion of playing games on television screens. I was waiting at a bus stop and there was this advertising billboard of an all-American family gathered round their tv set, smiling like they were zonked out in some sort of blissful trance. By then millions and millions of Americans had brought television into their homes, and for many of us it was the centre of family life.

I set out my idea in a four-page proposal in the hopes I could get some research and development funding, and I remember thinking, hey, I'm in a military electronics corporation, and this has nothing to do with the military, so how do I stop the bosses getting turned off? How do I make it sound like it applies to whatever the hell I'm supposed to be working on?

Well, I figured that it was all about the intent, so I had to keep right away from words that made it all sound like I wanted to produce toys and playthings for the good citizens at home. And there was one word that the military used all the time for training and simulations, and that word was "gaming". Once I'd worked that one out, I applied my concept to the good old profit motive, and I outlined how gaming on home screens could be a great commercial proposition. You probably expect me to claim that I coined the name Gamers for my tv-based players, in which case it was me who I coined the title of this book. And you would be one hundred per cent right. That was in 1966, and this time my bosses were interested, but only to the tune of a lousy $2,500 for the project.

In less than a year, and with the help of a technician guy called Bob Tremblay, we came up with a test unit codename TV Game Unit #1. It was real primitive and had a basic alignment generator built in. As a result there was just a dot on the screen that the viewer could control manually, but it worked. Then Billy Harrison and Bill Rusch joined in the fun, and we managed to build more and more sophisticated units, with some more graphics and two-player controls, until one day the top brass said to me, OK Ralph, just go for it, just make this into a product that people want to buy.

Believe me, it wasn't a quick job, and it wasn't easy either, in fact it took me and my team four or five years to get it right. But eventually, at the seventh attempt, we came up with the first viable multiplayer, multiprogram video game system, and I called it the Brown Box. The world's first games console was called the Brown Box after the brown parcel tape we wrapped it in to simulate wood veneer.

We touted it round a whole mess of companies, who all turned it down, but then in 1972, Sanders Associates licensed my Brown Box to Magnavox, who packaged it all up and released it as the Magnavox Odyssey. To tell the truth it was a pretty weird hybrid product, but at the time it was revolutionary. If you know the expression that a camel is a horse designed by a committee, then in that case the Odyssey was one hell of a camel. It had a brown, black and white plastic box that connected direct to the TV aerial socket, and a pair of controllers attached by wires, each with a vertical and horizontal knob and an action-button. Then there was a choice of twelve colour overlays to hang on the front of the tv screen to simulate each gameplay: Table Tennis, Tennis, Hockey, Football, Ski, Submarine, Haunted House, Analogic, Cat and Mouse, Roulette, States and Simon Says. What I mean is you literally had to hang those transparent sheets over the front of your TV and pretend they were part of the on-screen action.

In reality the gameplay was all the same, and that was because the Odyssey could only generate three little square dots and one variable line. And it was really dumb, as in totally. It couldn't track any movements or scores, it didn't do anything that wasn't hard-wired into memory, and there was no audio at all. In other words it wasn't much of a sexy commercial proposition for Mister and Missus America to spend their dollars on. So what we decided to do was to throw in some paper money and a dice to jazz things up, as well as a cheap little booklet to flesh out the gameplay. Later on we sold the first video-game light gun as an extra, which was neat, and which really did spawn a whole new type of gaming at home and in the arcades. So that's two things you can thank me for, the name for you Gamers and the peripheral doo-dab that became known as the add-on.

After the Odyssey, I took out a raft of patents, around 150 of them in fact, and I reckon they must have kept the lawyers in business for the next twenty years, including what one judge called "the pioneering patent of the video game." And that's why it's my ghost that's in this book and not some other guy, and if you reckoned Nolan Bushnell thought up *Pong*, take a look at *Table Tennis* on the Magnavox Odyssey. Then take a look at US Patent Number 3728480, baby.

Ralph Baer, 1972
Courtesy of the Ralph Baer Collection,
American Classic Arcade Museum, Laconia

☐DYSSEY™

TURNS ANY TV,* BLACK AND WHITE OR COLOR, INTO AN ELECTRONIC GAME CENTER!

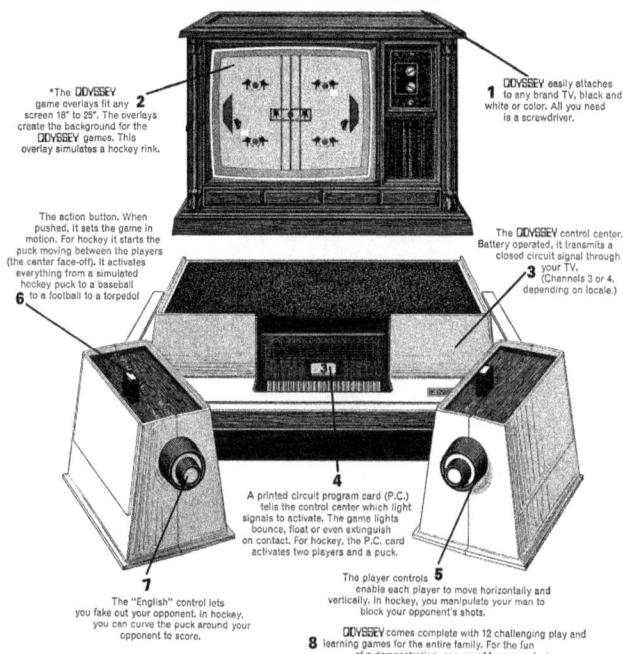

*The ☐DYSSEY **2** game overlays fit any screen 18" to 25". The overlays create the background for the ☐DYSSEY games. This overlay simulates a hockey rink.

☐DYSSEY easily attaches **1** to any brand TV, black and white or color. All you need is a screwdriver.

The action button. When pushed, it sets the game in motion. For hockey it starts the puck moving between the players (the center face-off). It activates everything from a simulated hockey puck to a baseball **6** to a football to a torpedo!

The ☐DYSSEY control center. Battery operated, it transmits a closed circuit signal through your TV. **3** (Channels 3 or 4, depending on locale.)

4 A printed circuit program card (P.C.) tells the control center which light signals to activate. The game lights bounce, float or even extinguish on contact. For hockey, the P.C. card activates two players and a puck.

7 The "English" control lets you fake out your opponent. In hockey, you can curve the puck around your opponent to score.

The player controls **5** enable each player to move horizontally and vertically. In hockey, you manipulate your man to block your opponent's shots.

8 ☐DYSSEY comes complete with 12 challenging play and learning games for the entire family. For the fun of a demonstration, see your Magnavox dealer.

TABLE TENNIS TENNIS HOCKEY FOOTBALL SKI SUBMARINE HAUNTED HOUSE ANALOGIC CAT AND MOUSE ROULETTE STATES SIMON SAYS

Magnavox

PARENTS'

THE MAGNAVOX COMPANY • 1700 MAGNAVOX WAY, FORT WAYNE, INDIANA 46804

Magnavox Odyssey publicity, 1972
Courtesy of the Ralph Baer Collection,
American Classic Arcade Museum, Laconia

The Thirteenth Ghost

Jerry Lawson 1940-2011

The Games Cartridge, 1976

Hi there, everybody. This is Jerry Lawson, and I'm the guy who brought you the video-game cartridge. So I guess I'm also the guy who laid the foundation for today's multi-billion dollar gaming industry. They say I kickstarted gaming's fast-track evolution for all you gamers, so if that's the case then welcome to my story.

I was born in Brooklyn, New York City on New Year's Day 1940. My grandaddy dreamed of being a physicist, but things were like they were back then and he made it as far as a postmaster. My mom was a hard worker and she was big on the local PTA. Yep, she was a real fierce lady. And my daddy was a longshoreman loading and unloading those old cargo ships at the dockside. What my mom and daddy had in common was they wanted me to have the best education I could. Their hero was a great scientist name of George Washington Carver, who was of the negro race. Even in our society today we don't seem to celebrate a whole load of black ghosts, but here I am anyways and I'll begin at the beginning.

I guess I was a smart kid. I went and built my own radio station at home and got me my amateur radio licence before I was fourteen years old. By then I was living in Queens, which had the most ethnic variation on the planet with everyone living cheek by jowl. I got in to Queens College, but I had to drop out so as I could earn some money from repairing TV sets all round the neighbourhood. Then I got in to the City College of New York, but I didn't make it through to a degree there either because I quit. I had taught myself as much as I could about electronics and engineering and I reckoned I knew more than my teachers by then. At least, I knew enough to go looking for the main chance.

The electronics action was starting to happen on the other side of the nation in California, and my folks backed my decision to move out there from Queens, even though they knew I'd be a lone black face among all the rest. They told me not to be afraid of my background but to celebrate it. And that's what I did. I strutted my stuff and I joined a club.

So let me tell you about the Homebrew Computer Club. We met up in what's now Silicon Valley, actually we used to meet up in the parking lot of the Safeway store, which was the nearest venue to the university campus. Then the club meetings moved to The Oasis Bar, and on to a pub on El Camino Real in Menlo Park.

When I joined, we were a wild bunch of hackers, gamers and would-be entrepreneurs, people like Adam Osborne who designed the first portable computer, Harry Garland who launched Cromemco, Fred Moore the civil rights activist, Roger Melen who gave us colour graphics, Captain Crunch the original phone phreaker, George Morrow the champion of the S-100 bus, Paul Terrell founder of Byte Shop, Lisa Loopy Strauss who designed the Atari 800, Li-Chen Wang the author of Tiny BASIC, Dan Werthimer the founder of the Search for Extra-Terrestrial Intelligence, oh yeah, and there were a couple of guys called Steve Jobs and

Steve Wozniak. I wonder if those two ever came up with anything worthwhile! Anyway, we talked the talk and we drank a whole lot of beer.

The Club newsletter was the biggest force in Silicon Valley culture, I reckon, and we all took a hand editing it. We helped our members build their original kit computers like the Altair, and most of us were really into gaming. Oh yeah, and we published something called the *Open Letter to Hobbyists* from a young whippersnapper called Bill Gates who wanted to use our magazine to take a pop against software piracy.

As for me, I landed at Fairchild Semiconductors over in San Francisco as a field engineer, a kind of applications troubleshooter in their sales division. That was in 1970 as far as I recall, and that was where I heard about a coin-op games machine called *Pong*, which had been set up in a beer hall and pizza parlour in Sunnyvale. And I'm not sure if it was a rip-off of Ralph Baer's *Table Tennis* on the Magnavox, but I'll leave his ghost to fight that one out. They said that some local jocks had rigged a low voltage wired gadget to shock the *Pong* machine and trigger it to spill its guts of all the coins inside so they could steal them, and I thought that was kind of neat. In fact I got inspired to create my own coin-op video game right there in my garage. I used Fairlight's latest F8 microprocessor and I called my game *Demolition Derby*, making damn sure I built in a defeat mode against coin theft. It may have been the earliest microprocessor game ever, I don't know for sure, but what I do know is that it was never released.

By then *Pong* was a smash hit all over the land, and I ran into its engineering creator Al Alcorn, known as Employee Number 3 at Atari. He had been on the lookout for the latest electronic components from us at Fairchild, and I was the go-to guy. They sent me out to meet Al and explain how our product worked, and I guess I helped him out. We became friends for a while. Well, sort of friends, because we also became competitors in the same gaming world. I think

Al used to call me his frenemy whenever he was asked, and I'm sad if he thinks I ripped off his ideas. I didn't, what I did do was to leapfrog over them.

My bosses at Fairchild got the tip-off that I was doing a bit of side work with Al Alcorn, and instead of firing me they got me to swear to secrecy and start up a games project in-house instead. That's business for you.

It was in 1975 that I became Director of Engineering and Marketing for Fairchild's new video game division, and that was at a time when every games system had the software preprogrammed and built into the hardware casing. Ralph Baer had given us the games console, but the gamer couldn't swap anything or play the latest games that weren't already built in. If a gamer tried to crack the case to load new software they'd either ruin the console or get an electric belt up the arm and straight into the heart. I thought that was nuts, and what gamers needed was a safe alternative. All the technology was there, but it was just that no sucker had figured out how to apply it. Even all those university geeks in the Homebrew Computer Club didn't see it, and it took this dropout from Brooklyn to deliver. A year later, when I invented the games console, I guess I made history. But not without help.

There were these two guys over at the Alpex Computer Corporation, name of Larry Haskel and Wallace Kirschner, and they'd just developed a really neat computer memory cartridge. Read-only-memory, that is, a matchbox size ROM cartridge. I licensed their little yellow plastic prototype for Fairchild, and soon as I had the paperwork signed I set about designing a machine round it using our own microprocessor, the F8.

My idea was to store any kind of new games on removable cartridges, so the gamer could slot them in and yank them out whenever they wanted. No cracked cases. No electric shocks. And as Director of Engineering and Marketing I recognised that this could be the start of a whole load of new revenue streams for programmers, designers, packagers, marketers, wholesalers, retailers and distributors at one end, and collectables for gamers at the other. We called our first video game console the Fairchild Channel F, but I soon found out that integrating the cartridge was the easy bit.

The gaming joysticks and controllers at the time were lousy up-down-left-right affairs, so I went and designed a brand new joystick with an 8-way controller, and that allowed designers and players a whole load more scope and control. I also integrated the very first Pause-control on any games machine, so gamers could go for a smoke or take a leak and restart exactly where they left off. If I'm going to be remembered by gamers at all, then I'd like to be remembered for that too.

Well, I got hit by problem after problem, and managed to solve them all, except one. The goddam Federal Communications Commission blocked their approval to market our Channel F console because it failed their radiation signal test, and no matter any which way I tried I couldn't make the damn thing compliant. I was lying awake in the early hours trying to figure it out when I had an epiphany moment like those three guys in the Bible. I phoned up my team and asked them to leave their nice warm beds and get over to the office asap, and you know something, every one of them did. When we were all gathered together I said I'd come up with the way how to reduce the radiation, but I just couldn't do the calculation and needed help.

It was teamwork that solved it, and it all came down to shrinking the length of the controllers as short as possible down to a stunted little joystick. It worked, and I took our modified machine to the Federal Commission in person, where I sat in their goddam lobby for three straight days until they surrendered and gave their approval. I guess I was a real tenacious son of a bitch.

And if you think that was a happy ending, then I'm sorry to disappoint you. The Fairchild Channel F bombed. I don't really know why, but it was a commercial flop. It looked great, it worked great, the titles were great, but maybe it was just a fraction ahead of its time when we launched at the Chicago CES in the June of 1976. Just over a year later, Atari launched its 2600 model, and we all know how that stormed the market. And I give credit where credit's due, the man responsible for the Atari was my old frenemy Al Alcorn.

Yeah, well, I jumped ship and quit Fairchild to start up my own company that I called Videosoft, making games for Atari. Aw, come on now. Like I say, business is business, guys. And at least my 8-way joystick idea got taken up for later Atari models. So here I am, haunting every games cartridge ever made, so you can play hundreds of individual titles on a single platform. I'm the guy who unlocked the doors to selling hundreds of millions of games, and that's something to be proud of.

And that's the end of my gaming story. Sure, I did other stuff, like working with Stevie Wonder on the Wonder Clock for kids, like mentoring gamers at Stanford, like getting the Gerald A Lawson Academy of Arts named for me, like winning the Xbox Gaming Heroes Award, like slowly losing bits off of me before I died from diabetes. That's about it. Hope you remember me, folks. It was a life.

Jerry Lawson, 1980
photographer unknown, Museumofplay.org
photo of historical significance, low resolution copyright-free usage

Fairlight Channel F game consoles and cartridges, 1976
with thanks for use to Goodwill Gamer, r/gamecollecting archive

The Fourteenth Ghost

Alice Wonderwoman Washington
1947-2017

The Coin-op Revolution, 1980

I got a question. Why am I in this book? I wasn't famous and what I did for gaming was way behind the scenes. I tell you what I think. I think I'm put in this book so the cover looks PC, as in politically correct. Like, hey gamer dudes, look at the black chick in sunglasses with the big wide smile, this book ain't all about miserable old white men. That's what I think. Sure, my story follows on from Jerry Lawson, the only other person of color who makes the grade, but me, really?

Besides, I don't want to talk about me anyways, I'd rather discuss the whole business of black people in gaming. You hear what I'm saying? Do you care where I was born and where I was raised and what my momma gave me for my food? I'm only talking on condition I stay away from all that and write what I want. That's the deal, and you can take it or leave it.

So I worked at Atari California, and they called me Wonderwoman. Atari was in Sunnyvale, in the business park. That was in '78, maybe it was '79. They had this blonde girl at reception, so as not to scare folks off. White desk, white telephone, white everything, 'cept the logo and that was blood red. I was in the coin-op assembly, Borregas Avenue. That's all gone now, tore down by Google after they bought everything they could lay their hands on.

Back when I was there, there was zero black faces in senior management. Black faces were on the shop floor, sure we were. We got paid less too. Goes without saying that if there's no diversity in the industry that'll lead to no diversity in the games. Those days in the games there was more green faces with horns on than black faces, and there ain't much as has changed, at least not much last time I took a peek at gaming these days. The default skin color in today's games is almost always light-tone, and when African-American males do make an appearance they're either all sweated up doing sports or acting lawless and aggressive. As for us black women, hah, we're mostly props or hookers or victims.

You want stats? I got stats. In your top-rated games there's only 3% of the main characters which are black. No surprise to me at all. New research on street games and action-shooters says that black characters get portrayed as brutal, casual criminal and sexually promiscuous. Let me tell you, I was none of that, and same goes for the brothers and sisters I knew and I worked with.

And don't get me started. The International Game Developers Association says thirteen per cent of our country identifies as black or Afro-Caribbean, so how come only two per cent actually work in the gaming industry today? There's a mighty big turn off going on somewheres.

Me? People say I was a pioneering figure in the gaming industry, in fact they said I was the crucial figure, and that's because what I did was put every single thing you need onto a PCB, that's a printed circuit board, and install it in every Atari coin-op machine. When I say every single thing on one board, I don't just mean the game, I mean all the tech you need to run that game as well. It made playing the coin-ops a really smooth experience, and it cut out all the costs of itsy-bitsy assembly and relays and wiring. Sure, it was probably the single thing that made gaming so popular not just in the States, but all over the world.

The only real recognition I ever got was in the Atari newspaper, but hey that's the way it goes. They wrote, "Alice Washington was poetry in motion. Power drill in one hand, printed circuit board in the other, she installed the PC board in the cabinet in a few seconds flat. Almost as an afterthought she placed a cover on the games on-off switch and stuck a safety label on the power cord." That's it people, that's what I got.

And I guess it's up to me to give a shout out to my team, so I will. First the gaming cabinets were made in the wood shop, then they got moved to the paint shop next door for silkscreening the outside images. Then the real fun began, when the cabinets came to us to assemble the guts. The production controller was Mike Vasquez, who looked like a latino movie star. Raquel Garcia and Gertrude Schwalbe handled the sheetmetal brackets, the lights and the game panels. It didn't take them longer than ten minutes to assemble each unit. The TV displays were real heavy and they came in overhead on a sort of ski lift, and got adjusted by a long-hair called Jeff Atchison, for focus and brightness, and for color too. After I installed my PCBs for the actual game, Karen Jay was in charge of the final assembly all ready for the packers Mike Govier and Gino Ortez to seal them up and load them onto the truck. I guess there was ten stations on that assembly line, and our games machines rolled off really really fast. I can't remember who first started calling me Wonderwoman, but I didn't mind it one bit.

Let me tell you about the all-time favourite game that I did, called *Gravatar*, and that one was in 1982. We turned out way over five thousand of them. It was a shooter designed by Mike Hally and programmed by Rich Adam. Brad Chaboya did the cabinet art, and I loved it. I'd say it was the last of the classic arcade color-vector titles, and after that, well, I'll get on to what happened. It had the same rotate and thrust controls as the original *Asteroids*, but it was real hard to play. There was a whole solar system to navigate your rocket through, and gravity played a major part in the gameplay. That meant the player had to very very precise and careful with all the controls.

There were five buttons for shoot, rotate left, rotate right, thrust and one for the tractor-beam and force field. There were enemy bunkers, fuel tanks, reactors, and all sorts of new solar systems and universes with changing views and perspectives. I really liked it when the gravity effect got reversed, and instead of getting dragged towards the surface of a planet your rocket got pushed away like by an invisible hand of god. It was so hard to play that Mike and Rich never managed to complete their own game. Well, not without cheating!

I remember going to see a James Bond movie, where Kim Basinger is meeting up with Double-O-Seven in a casino in Monte Carlo, and she looks like a million dollars playing my *Gravatar* machine. And you know something else, I'm a ghost in Tesla electric cars too, because in 2019 *Gravatar* was added to their onboard entertainment system. But that's now and then was then, and in 1983 we had the video game crash. In Japan they called it the Atari Shock. I won't put into print what I called it, but I didn't use pretty words. The market just got saturated, and there were just too many games out there, mostly real bad quality. And the coin-ops cost money and the arcades got empty when the boom in personal home computers came in. We called the time before the crash The Golden Age, and I helped make it happen, and then it all came to an end.

If you're interested in *Gravatar* some more, a guy called Ray Mueller set a world record in 1982 with a score of

4,722,200 after playing 12 hours 21 minutes. He was either a hero or he was nuts. And his record wasn't broken until 2006 with Dan Coogan scoring 8,029,450 when he played for 23 hours and fifteen minutes. I'm not going to tell you what I think about game addiction, someone else can use their chapter to do that, but a word to any other "pioneer in video gaming", you just beware of unintended consequences, hear what I'm saying.

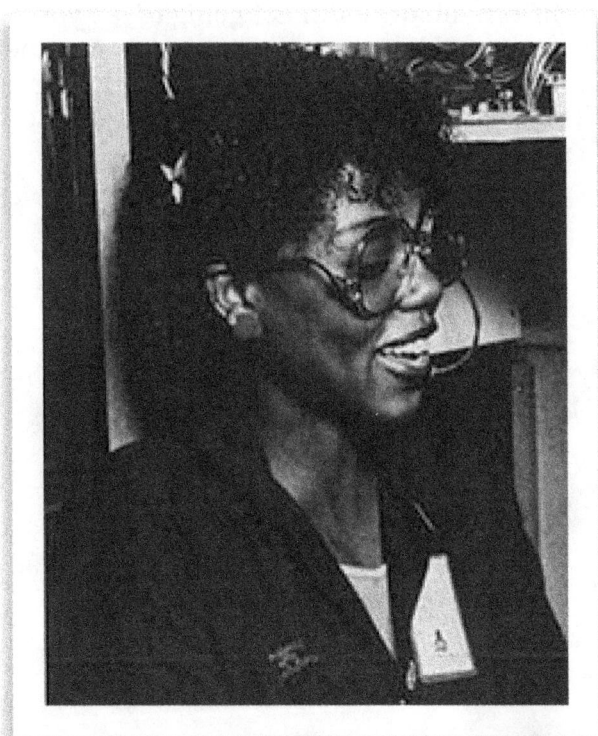

Alice Wonderwoman Washington, 1982
with thanks for publication usage to The Strong, Rochester, New York

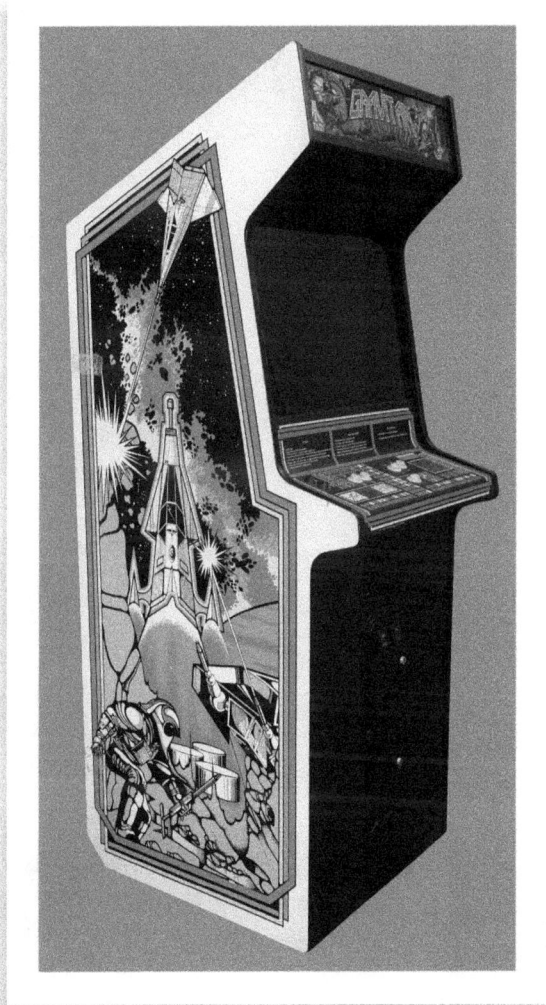

Gravitar arcade cabinet, 1982

The Fifteenth Ghost

Gunpei Yokoi 1949-1998

The Handheld, 1980

I am Gunpei Yokoi, but you may know me as Mister Nintendo, or the Game Boy Man, and some people call me the Father of Video Games, but I have always thought of myself merely as a good toy maker. I have been the ghost in your handheld games machines since I died in 1998 which is when I became a *Yokai*, as we call ourselves in Japanese folklore. Some of our ghosts are malevolent, some create mischief and some can be benevolent, so I hope you think of me as one of the benevolent ones. We *Yokai* are not shimmery spectres like the ghosts in Western cultures, we prefer to have distinct forms such as humanoid animals or familiar objects, but in my opinion the most interesting of us are the shapeshifters, the *obake*. It is this shapeshifting that has been central to my life in gaming.

I was a student at Doshisha University in the beautiful city of Kyoto, and when I graduated with a degree in electronics I was hired by Nintendo to maintain an assembly line for the manufacture of *hanafuda*, which are like small playing cards. The line had been going for over seventy years when I arrived there in 1965.

One day, when I was quite new in the factory, Nintendo's boss, the great Hiroshi Yamauchi, had made a business deal with Walt Disney to licence cartoon characters for themed cards printed on plastic, and when he came to inspect the production line he spotted something unusual. It was a toy trash-picker, a little plastic extending arm that I had made for my own amusement. Well, the Boss immediately commissioned me to get my novelty toy into production in time for Christmas, and we called it the *Ultra Hand*. It didn't actually do anything except reach out and grab things, but I added a pair of little bowl-shaped grips and bundled three coloured balls with miniature stands in the package. To cut a very short story even shorter, we sold over a million units in no time at all, and I became the Boss's go-to boy. My fate was sealed.

I thoroughly enjoyed the next stage of my toy-making career and conceived all sorts of novelties. My *Chiritory* was a cute little remote-control vacuum cleaner, the *Ultra Machine* threw baseballs around like a demented child, the *Ten Billion Barrel* was rather like a circular Rubik's Cube puzzle, and then Nintendo's leap into the electronics gaming world came in 1969 when I designed my *Love Tester*. I think that one is still going strong today!

The *Love Tester* was a two-player novelty the size of a modern cellphone with a pair of spherical sensors connected to the device by wires. The idea was that each partner in a couple held their sphere in one hand, then completed the electric circuit by holding each other's free hand. Depending on the electrical resistance, their Love Score got displayed on the device on a scale between 1 and 100. I used to have a lot of fun telling players that their score would increase if they kissed with their mouths open. The *Love Tester* was the first Nintendo device that we sold outside of Japan, and from then on it seemed I could do no wrong in the eyes of the company. And the fact was, I couldn't.

One day, I was travelling to a meeting on the bullet train at two hundred miles an hour, and I happened to observe a businessman in the same carriage who was relieving the boredom of his journey by playing with an electronic calculator, one of the pocket kind with a little LCD display. I noticed how he was oblivious to everything around him, and fixated on the results of stabbing at the buttons on the keypad. I have no idea if he was playing numbers games, or just seeing how many English words he could mimic by turning the display upside down to form **HELLO** with **07734**, or the juvenile practice of making your calculator say **BOOBS** with **58008**. Whatever he was doing, he not only changed my life, he also gave me the idea that changed the lives of millions of gamers. Because it was then that I conceived of a hand-held clock that could double up as a personal video-game device. But I did not develop the idea any further and I put it to the back of my mind until several months later.

I used to drive a left-hand-drive import car, and it so happened that the President of Nintendo used a chauffeur-driven Cadillac which was also left-hand-drive. Well, one day his chauffeur went down with a heavy cold and didn't turn up for duty to drive the Boss to a meeting at the Osaka Plaza Hotel, and there was nobody available who had experience of driving American cars. So the head of personnel came to me and said, "I'm very sorry to ask this, Yokoi, but would you mind being the President's driver just for today?" I wasn't some lowly driver, I was the chief of development, but I swallowed my pride and during the drive I got to talking about that day when I watched the salaryman playing with his calculator on the bullet train.

"I think it could be really interesting if we made a little calculator-sized game console," I told him. "Up to now, our philosophy with toys has been that the bigger they are, the better they sell, but I think a calculator-size game device would allow even salarymen like us to play games discreetly."

The President didn't react at all, and seemed

unimpressed by my idea, but it turned out that his meeting was with President Saeki of the Sharp Corporation, the leading calculator manufacturer in the world. About a week later, one of Sharp's top executives arrived at our offices and he seemed very excited, but I had no idea why until the Boss informed me that we were going full speed ahead with my idea. So I guess it was down to his chauffeur having a head cold that led to the development of the handheld gaming revolution. I guess in this life, timing is everything, as it is in death.

Japanese salarymen were very conservative then, as I suspect they still are, and they would have been far too embarrassed to whip out a games machine on a bullet-train or anywhere else for that matter. It would not be socially acceptable for a grown man. So I set about designing a device that could be played as discreetly as possible. When a salaryman is seated on a train he habitually holds his hands above his lap, so I designed my games unit to be played in that modest position. The most comfortable option would be to use both thumbs to control the gameplay, and that led to the positioning of control buttons for horizontal playing rather than vertical. I decided that as well as a simple game, my device should also function as a digital clock, allowing the salaryman to appear serious and businesslike if the need arose and he wished to hide his gaming.

My appropriately named *Game & Watch* was released on April 28, 1980, and as well as the digital clock it ran a little game called *Ball*. We hoped that it might eventually sell 100,000 units, and ease our struggling cashflow at Nintendo. In fact, *Ball* was in production for over ten years, and we sold 43.4million units. But the life of *Game & Watch* was almost stifled at birth, and the history of gaming could have been very different.

The Boss instructed me to keep my focus on my novelty toys, and he took the project away from me and handed it over to the Nintendo team that dealt with TV games. They flatly declared that my concept was far too difficult to bring to market, and scrapped it. So I just carried on with it solo in my spare time. I created a mock up of *Ball* by shining lights through cut-out paper shapes, and showed it to my friend and colleague Satoru Okada, who went and taught himself how to program for an Intel 8080 and then designed the electronics himself. We took it along to Sharp direct, who also rejected the prototype saying it couldn't be scaled down to the size of a calculator, but we just left our prototype with them and said they could play with it for their own amusement. And it amused them enough to change their minds.

Before *Game & Watch*, I don't believe Sharp had considered using LCD screens for anything except calculators, and they had been in fierce competition with Casio who were steaming ahead in the market. The Sharp liquid-crystal factories were in decline and there was a surplus of LCDs just waiting to be repurposed, so as it turned out our timing couldn't have been better. I don't think it's an exaggeration to say that my device brought them back from the edge of extinction.

Of course the Boss did a complete U-turn, and gave me the green light for three new games for *Game & Watch*, and then another three, and then another three, until eventually I personally devised ofter fifty of them. Some were little masterpieces I think, *Manhole, Fire, Turtle Bridge*, and then on to projects like *Donkey Kong* and *Mario*. I was no longer designing for the salaryman on the bullet train. The public attitude towards hand-held gaming soon shifted and it was no longer a habit that needed concealment, nor was it something that was restricted to one generation. Kids were the new mass market.

The basic elements of the gameplay in my titles soon became exhausted, that was inevitable, and as a result I became more interested in exaggerating the absurd and creating weird and wonderful backgrounds. I was provided with a great many inspirations from the world of anime, but my inspirations from that world were of the humour and the surreal side as opposed to the heroic and violent. So it was unfortunate that my own ending was of the violent kind.

I was being driven on the Hokuriku Expressway which runs along Japan's Northern coastline, when the traffic slowed down and before we could stop we shunted into the rear end of the vehicle in front. It was a shiny new truck, and the driver was not happy at all. I got out to inspect the damage when a car driven by a tourist representative called Gen Tsushima came up behind in the middle lane and killed me.

And that is why I am a *Yokai*, a happy shape-shifter just like a character in one of my own games. It has been a pleasure telling you my little story, and I hope you enjoyed the experience.

Gunpei Yokoi, 1996
with thanks to Yokogao photographic archive, Tokyo. Public domain

Game & Watch, Ball, 1980

The Sixteenth Ghost

Mike Johnston 1948-1991

Mainstream Gaming, 1981

H ello everyone. You can call me Father Christmas. It's what hordes of young gamers often used to call me. But before I begin, I would like to dedicate my Chapter in this worthy book to my inspirational chum Tim Hartnell, who died at almost the same time I myself departed your land of the living. He was only 40 and I was only 43.

But I have no room for melancholy here, because my story is a joyous one, and I am comfortable with the fact that very few people know it. An online search on Tim Hartnell will spew out hundreds of items, more like thousands, whereas a search on my name will deliver a drummer in Folsom California and a politician in Denver Colorado, but certainly not yours truly. I was something quite different, I was an accidental hero, and an unsung one too. I was midwife to the home-grown videogame industry born right here in the UK, and from here in the UK it went on to spread all over the world. From bedrooms to billions.

If you need to picture me at all, then please picture me as a rather tall, rather plump bespectacled Englishman working for Her Majesty Queen Elizabeth at the Ministry of Pencils and Paperclips, with a fag in one hand and a bottle of red in the other, checked shirt, cord trousers, tweed jacket, all rumpled and jolly, and topped off with a deerstalker hat. Now grow me a magnificent set of whiskers and plant a huge smile in the middle of them. That's me.

But that wasn't always me. Once I was a baby-boomer, vintage 1948, when my post-war dreams were nurtured by free milk, free orange juice, free rose-hip syrup, free cod liver oil, free education and the blessed free National Health Service. Truly it was a paradise to live in the England of our beloved leader the great Clement Attlee. Apart from the impetigo and the nits, of course.

Like the other post-war kids, I played my fair share of games, although I favoured chess and *Ludo* over boxing and football. My early interest in electronic entertainment was more to do with numbers and logic than with gaming, but thanks to my height and gregarious manner I could pass as an adult and get into the pub a few years before I was legally entitled.

Ah, the pub! The nicotine-stained walls and ceilings, the heady perfume of stale beer and Victorian toilets. The sticky carpets and peeling anaglypta. The frosted glass windows steamed up in order to hide interior sin and depravity from exterior passers-by. The crisps, the nuts, the pork scratchings. The cigarette machine, the *Durex* machine, the pinball machine, the one-arm bandit machine, and above all the electronic games machine.

Periscope arrived at the London Amusement Trades Exhibition in 1966 and then into the pub, but it was the arrival of *Pong* that started the gaming revolution in my neck of the woods, and in July 1973 our local *Pong* machine was appropriately placed next to the aroma of the pub toilet. One outfit, by the name of Dormer Projects, boasted they had installed over 5,000 units of Atari's *Pong* games machines in pubs and clubs throughout the UK by the Christmas of that year. They cost around £650 a pop, and on average they were relieving gamers of £80 a week at each site, so it was the investor's money back in the first two months then profit all the way. And, my friends, that set me to thinking.

In 1979 a new electronic game appeared in the pub, and it really pissed off the old boys who wanted to drink their real ale in a traditional Happy Hour ambience of moans and misery. It was called *Space Invaders* and it was noisy! It was also hungry, swallowing ten-pee pieces at a rate of knots. And that set me to thinking even more. It was a time when home micros were starting to appear. The Acorn, the Compukit, Tangerine's Microtan, the Nascom, Commodore Pet, and in February 1980 a home computer kit, selling for less than a hundred quid, called the Sinclair ZX80. I was a thirty-one year old civil servant living near the Tottenham football stadium and I had been thinking far too long. It was time for action!

I joined something called the National ZX80 Users Club, which had been set up by Tim Hartnell, an Australian writer who lived in London not far from me over in Earls Court. The Club may have been called National, but in reality we were only a handful of computer and gaming enthusiasts. I suggested to Tim that we should organise a get-together in the pub to press the flesh of our members, and he agreed. So he announced the time, date and venue in the club newsletter, and we waited clutching our pints to see if we could spot any likely fellow-geeks. I was completely amazed when around seventy of the buggers turned up, and crowded out the room. The landlady was absolutely delighted, and she must have turned a tidy profit that night. As I recall, most of the conversations were about which RAM pack was the best value, but I was pleasantly surprised by the number of gamers there.

I learned from that pub meeting that most of our members were interested in creating and playing games on their micros, but they only seemed to swap hints and tips with one another. They did not see it as a money-spinner. The games software industry didn't exist back then, it was for hobbyists only. There were bedroom software producers who were swapping and selling their creations, and a few of them had set up commercially using amateur talent. But there were no market stalls, no gaming shops, no retailers, no wholesalers, no agents, no distributors, in fact no parasites at all. Everything was done by word of mouth and via newsletters like ours, and I reckoned I could fill the gap. Ho! Ho! Ho!

Those first commercial game producers had started to take out adverts in the early enthusiast magazines and were happy to use mail-order to sell their wares, which were duplicated onto audio cassettes and accompanied by rudimentary paper inserts. But it was obvious there were more enthusiasts around than we knew about, so the question was how to reach out to them. I told Tim that I reckoned we could increase the scale of our next meeting by including the people who actually created the games, because this would allow for proper communication between the software authors and the gamers who enjoyed their wares.

Tim agreed, but he was full-time writing and fannying about with book publishing, so I volunteered to organise the next meeting, and I decided that I would become an exhibitionist on a grand scale, not aiming at dozens of gamers, but hundreds. My first step was deciding how best to attract an audience, and the answer seemed obvious; I would advertise in the same magazine where those game producers were trying to sell their titles. But there was only one problem. I didn't have any money. I would have to beg, borrow and steal.

Seeing that our newsletter had a circulation of around 450, and we had attracted seventy living breathing people to meet up, imagine if I took out an advert in a magazine with a circulation of a few thousand. That magazine was called *Popular Computing Weekly*. I calculated that with a bit of luck and a following wind I could haul in maybe 500 punters for a grand games meeting at a London venue with good travel links. And if I charged a small fee for software producers to hawk their games as well as charging gamers for entry tickets, then I might be able to make a profit that would keep me in fags and booze for several weeks. I settled on charging the kids fifty pee to get in, and their mums and dads a quid. To be honest, I didn't think any mums would turn up at all, and that was the only prediction I got right about the whole enterprise.

There were probably less than a hundred people producing leisure software back then, trying to sell it to a market they weren't sure existed. I knew quite a few of them and contacted some home-grown software pioneers to sound out my idea, and they seemed interested in renting out a trestle table to flog their hand-duplicated cassettes direct to gamers. I may have exaggerated the numbers that I expected to attend, but the rental price I proposed was ridiculously low at twenty quid for a shaky wooden trestle table with enough space to display half a dozen racks of cassettes.

I thought a hall in Camden Town would be ideal, because it would be nice and bohemian and very cheap. Then I found myself believing my own propaganda as I embroidered my conversations with a few of those early software nutters. There was Dave Heelas of Dk'Tronics, Mike Lord who went on to write the ZX81 User Handbook and titles like *Doomdark's Revenge*, Mel Croucher who had founded the UK's first software house, and Nick Lambert who was the guy that launched Quicksilva, and they all said that if they promised to offer their titles at discount prices then I could be thinking bigger. I set my sights on the Central Hall near Westminster Abbey, which could pack in a thousand punters in one of its larger spaces, so I rented half of one of those spaces.

I appointed myself Organiser of this self-styled ZX Microfair at my mess of a home office, 71 Park Lane, Tottenham, London, near the Spurs football stadium. I had zero savings to rent the hall, and I blagged a quarter-page advert in *PCW* magazine. I set the date for the event as Saturday September 26th in the year of our Lord 1981. Then I asked every software outfit in the land to stump up a measly twenty quid to get my show on the road, and I am eternally grateful to those who actually did. I guess eternity is quite a ling time to give thanks for this ghost in the machine, but thank you anyway to BugByte, Quicksilva, DK'Tronics, Automata, Hewson, Control Technology, Macronics, Michael Orwin, Microgen, JRS, Artic, Richard Shepherd, Leisure Games, JK Greye, Si Hessel, Second Foundation, Digital Integration, Bridge, Algor, and that guy Pete in the big hat who didn't have any software but played his guitar and put an optimistic tips-jar on his stand. All in all, another two dozen exhibitors booked a table and paid on the day, so I was in business. Monkey business.

When the big day dawned and I got up early to peer out my window, it was absolutely pissing down with rain, and I feared the worst. Then the phone rang. It was Tim's unmistakable Aussie twang. "Good morning you fat bastard, are you awake?"

I moaned that I might have to flee the country if the weather didn't let up. I didn't think the civil service employed bankrupts.

"You better get over here sharpish, mate. I'm at Central Hall and it's, um, interesting."

"Oh Christ, what's happened? It's not even breakfast time."

"I know. And they're queuing round the bloody block!"

"Are you serious, old chap?"

"I'm always serious when I'm witnessing a miracle. It's incredible!"

"Blimey! How many is incredible?"

"Um, hundreds, maybe a thousand ..."

A thousand? Queueing! But Tim was wrong. By the time I got there were at least two thousand gamers soaked to the skin in the rain, literally queuing round the block, and it was a very big block indeed. When the numbers hit three thousand, we were forced to open the doors early. At five thousand, I asked the Hall's management if we could expand the space as well as extend the opening hours, and in order to prevent a riot they agreed. I recognised that something was happening which was not just incredible, but phenomenal. And the phenomenon was the birth of a brand new mass movement. Popular gaming!

More and more gamers tried to get in to the Hall, and the situation got totally out of hand, in fact it was a serious safety hazard. So I rushed outside and grabbed the nearest policeman. There were plenty around seeing as the Abbey and Parliament were close by. He came in, took one look, and climbed up onto a chair. Then he yelled for everyone to file out into the street and form an orderly queue until more space became available. That was when the laughter started, and it soon turned into chants and singing. I need not have panicked because there was no animosity at all, no aggro, no punch-ups, just a whole load of micro enthusiasts having a great time. It was brilliant.

That afternoon I managed to do a quick poll of exhibitors asking if they were up for a second Microfair. Most of them offered to pay me there and then for another table. Some booked multiple tables. Some confessed to having taken over a thousand quid at that first event, from the outstretched hands of happy punters, all in cash. Some said they had received offers from clubs and shops to stock their games on approval. Some boasted that scouts from European countries had placed orders for multiple units of their software with the intention to sell at their own events abroad. Some were already drunk and disorderly by way of celebration, but my good breeding prevents me from naming them.

I booked my second ZX Microfair at the same venue for Saturday January 30th 1982, by which time Sinclair Research, the manufacturer of the ZX micros, had become the world's leading brand in home computers. This time I planned for success, with a huge space and extended hours. But of course

I was still working full time for the Ministry of Pencils and Paperclips, so I politely asked anyone interested in exhibiting to phone me on my home number after seven in the evening to give me time to get back from work. Spaces sold out within a week of the announcement, and this time 12,000 gamers turned up, only gaining access on a one-in-one-out basis. I expanded my empire faster than my waistline, with more and more fairs at increasingly ambitious venues in different centres of population around England. I did everything solo and everyone seemed to want to be my best buddy.

Over a few short years I put on a couple of dozen ZX Microfairs, and gaming definitely went mainstream. High Street shops like WH Smith and Woolworths were stocking a range of videogames in serried ranks on their shelves, but there was no soul to that. My fairs were the only opportunity where gamers could meet the people who actually wrote and produced their favourites, and where they could get together with a mass of fellow enthusiasts and have some fun.

It was the Automata boys who provided most of that fun. I don't think they wanted to be in software at all, they wanted to be in showbiz. One time in Birmingham they didn't bother with any software but turned their stand into a stage for local bands to perform in. Another time, because there was no bar, they brought in barrels of beer and set up an old-time pub for a knees-up. Once they turned up with real gold and diamonds for a prize game with no security or insurance. They even put me on a track in one of their pop songs, I think it was called *Ally Pally Wally*. Ahem! And neither were they afraid to demonstrate against other exhibitors if they thought their software was misogynistic or ultra-violent. Nutters.

My favourite stunt of theirs was one time when the word went round that Revenue and Customs officers were in the hall, taking note of the cash that was being handled without any record or receipts. So Automata gave all their software away and then The PiMan, the Automata mascot who was their programmer Christian Penfold dressed in a skin-tight pink jumpsuit, commandeered the public address system and asked for the taxman to kindly make himself known so they could claim a tax rebate. Happy days. Happy days.

By the time of the 22nd Microfair staged at the Royal Horticultural Hall, I had upped the price of entry to a quid for the kids and one-and-a-kick for adults, which was still an absolute bargain, and I was feeling the pressure. I had taken on the job of production editor and consultant to a new magazine called *Sinclair User*, and somehow I had been elected as General Secretary of the Guild of Software Houses. So now even more people wanted to be my best buddy.

My best buddy since schooldays was a chap named Ed Murphy, whose son seemed to think I was the wizard Gandalf. Back then Ed lived in exotic Manchester City and I phoned him up one night to announce that I was putting on one of my Microfairs in Manchester and would love to pay him a visit and catch up. I said I had got a really good discount on the venue and told him the date. There was a long pause, then I heard him call his wife for a muttered conversation ending with, "Pauline, I think you'd better tell him." And tell me she did. I had arranged the Manchester Microfair for the day Pope John Paul was due to arrive in the city and play to an audience of a quarter of a million souls. Manchester would be utterly gridlocked, and if the Pope was infallible, then it was obvious that I wasn't. That Microfair was very far from a success.

One time Ed and Pauline came on a surprise visit to my place in London. I was delighted, but barred them from going into the sitting room because it was a little unsavoury. The washing machine had been kaput for some time, and I was storing my dirty laundry in there. In fact the room was full of black plastic bin liners stuffed with I know not what, and the atmospherics had gotten a wee bit rancid, but I didn't have any spare time to get the washer fixed or buy a new one, what with all the spreadsheets and organising of the

Microfairs. Besides I thought a new washing machine would cost a fortune.

They took one look at the machine, found the in-date warranty that had fallen behind it, and it was fixed the same day. Good people. In fact so good that they organised my funeral when my heart gave out. I'm happy to say that their son inherited my Sinclair ZX-80, so maybe I was Gandalf after all.

As for Tim, the last time I heard from him was when he told me he was going back to Oz, and he would be sure to let me know all about a guy called Angelo Cusumano. Tim said this guy was on a mission to popularise games software in Sydney.

"You better believe it Mike, the revolution you began in London is going to take over the world!"

"I don't think so, dear fellow," I replied, "I really don't think so."

But it turns out that Tim was right and I was wrong. If you are any sort of a popular gamer then somehow you are one of my beloved children. So bless you all.

upper: Mike Johnston with the author (left) and the PiMan (right)
lower: crowds at the Automata stand, ZX Microfair 1983
© Mel Croucher, private collection

ZX MICROFAIR

THERE'S ROOM FOR EVERYONE AT THE BIGGEST ZX MICROFAIR OF ALL TIME!

EVERYTHING FOR THE SPECTRUM, ZX81 AND MOST POPULAR MICROS!

BIG Twice as big as the last show!

BIG Even more exhibitors and interesting new computer products!

BIG Plenty of space to move, eat, drink and relax!

BIG Biggest value from any exhibition — admission £1 (50p for kids under 14)!

BIG Choice of hardware, software, books, peripherals, programs — even a bring-and-buy sale!

BIG Exhibition hall in parkland — big space — big car park!

BIG Big choice of "how to get there" — rail, road, bus, tube, foot — see right!

BIG Big day out for all the family!

BIG Big savings on most manufacturers' "show offers".

CUT OUT AND KEEP HOW TO GET TO THE BIG SHOW.

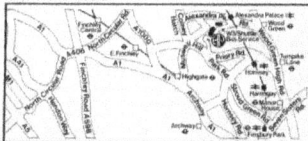

Come to the big one...

7th ZX MICROFAIR
ALEXANDRA PALACE, SATURDAY, JUNE 4th 1983

SATURDAY JUNE 4th at ALEXANDRA PAVILION, ALEXANDRA PALACE, WOOD GREEN, LONDON N22. FROM 10am to 6pm.
Advance tickets available from: Mike Johnston, 71 Park Lane, Tottenham, London N17 0HG. Adults £1.00. Kids (under 14) 50p.
Please make cheques payable to ZX MICROFAIR and enclose S.A.E.

Flyer for the 7th ZX Microfair 1983
Mel Croucher, private collection

The Seventeenth Ghost

Angelo Cusumano 1957–1995

The Game Store, 1982

G 'day, this is Angelo. They said my story was rags to riches, but there weren't any rags. Believe me. I'm not a whinger, so let me tell you this, when I finally hit the headlines Christmas 1995 it wasn't because I gave all you gamers a fair shake of the sauce bottle, it was because I got murdered by a flaming psycho. Let's go back to how it all started here in Sydney, Australia.

I met my darling Mary at a mate's wedding in 1977, and it was the old cliché of love at first sight. How wonderful is that. Mind you it took us four years to get hitched ourselves. We waited until we were a little bit older and settled enough to get married and spawn our ankle biters. The thing is, we got given this ripper TV for a wedding present, it was a Rank Arena, not one of the crook ones, but a brand new model that worked and I was stoked. The old models were made of rubbish components and they were always breaking down, but our one was indestructible and perfect for my favourite hobby, which was Atari gaming.

I loved my Atari 2600 almost as much as I loved my Mary, which was a lot. Our living room was full of games, stacks of them all around that colour tv. The pom Sinclair ZX81 had just arrived in Sydney, and there was this club downtown run by a bunch of dipsticks, going on about what was happening in London with thousands of gamers queuing round the block to get their mitts on the latest games at Mike Johnson's Microfairs. But like I say, I was an Atari console man. Those Sinclairs were for hobbyists farting around with tape decks, which was much too hard yakka for me.

I had a half decent background in electronics, and I reckoned I already understood the market. I could see the potential for making a living selling games and maybe getting to be a tall poppy, and Mary backed me up even though she didn't know much about gaming. What she did know was I wasn't afraid of hard work, and if a market didn't exist then I would bloody-well start building one. And she was a hard worker too. So I started up the first video game business in Oz, right there in the Sunday markets of Sydney. I didn't know anything about the video games business, of course, because there wasn't one. What I did know was that if a bloke like me was a gamer then there must be a load of others who would be if they could be.

Those Sunday markets were quite something. They were an institution. They were a proper day out. Families came in droves to have a good time and to hunt for bargains. So I hired a stall to see if anyone was interested in Atari games from an actual gamer who knew what he was talking about. And they were. Too right. It was ripper, and we sold out of everything we had. It was a family day out for us too. Not just Mary and me, but Angelo Junior, who would only have been about three back then. And then Chris the baby came along, and by the time Daniel was born things really took off. Our youngest, Deanna wasn't even a glint in my eye then, but don't let me get ahead of myself.

When I started it all, we worked from home, and the house got taken over and filled up with stock. We just about kept up. This pile of boxes would go to one market, that pile would go to another one. I started selling Intellivision games too. I got help and everyone came in to pick up their supplies for different markets. It was a toughie but I don't remember anyone ever spitting the dummy. Well, hardly ever. We were all one big family, no bludgers allowed, just hard workers. I thought we'd better get a name for the business, and the name seemed obvious. I called it The Gamesman. When the boys were old enough to join the business that changed to The Gamesmen plural, but like I say, let's not get ahead of ourselves.

By the end of 1982, we'd got a load of regular customers coming to the market stalls from all over the Big Smoke. "Stack 'em high and watch 'em fly" became my new slogan. It was the Sydney Easter Show that was the real biggie. Families would drive in from all over New South Wales for that one. It was more like a carnival, with this agricultural show chucked in, and of course stalls selling everything. Our exposure there was huge, and I decided to take a gamble and open a shop, so gamers would't have to wait for market days.

They say my Gamesman shop was the first dedicated computer-game store in the world. I dunno about that, but too right it was the first one in Bonds Road, Riverwood, Sydney. That was just as Nintendo hit big. I bloody loved it. I may have been half knackered, but everyone helped, including the boys as soon as they could. I found I had a knack for selling, and I invented a load of original pitches and slogans. "Computer games are our game!" That was one of mine that we used all the time.

It was perfect timing, because gaming popularity was steamrollering, specially for kids. They'd spend hours queuing up so they could check out the latest releases. I rigged up a row of machines and TVs for try-before-you-buy. Sega and Super Nintendo. I'd build these elaborate displays in the shop like a fake brick wall with Blanka busting through it for *Street Fighter*. Once I even made a real-looking helicopter for the launch of *Desert Strike* on the Mega Drive.

Then I started making radio jingles, "The Gamesmen's game is computer games," gamers would sing it as they came in the shop. Then as we opened more stores, the next move was obvious. In 1986 I started the TV commercials. All home made, with me, the kids and the displays in, but TV ads were pricey so we never did prime time. Later, everyone was doing that sort of thing, but back then we were unique, and I was the face and the voice of gaming. The youngsters would come in to the shop and point at me and say "Hey, look, it's the bloke off the tele!"

I was first in with mail order catalogues, and gave the postie a hernia. The catalogue came out every quarter, and it was stuffed with bundles, specials, tips, and come-ons to join the Gamesmen club. I worked silly hours to put those catalogues together. I sketched and photocopied and stuck the layouts together with glue, and my desk was chaos. But I always got the job done. 32 pages, maybe 250,000 copies by mail and letterbox drops. Even after I died Angelo Junior kept up the tradition and gave it a burl. He was the first to sell video games online. A real chip off the old block.

Right, let's get on to it. Thursday, twenty-first of December 1995, late night shopping with fifty or sixty customers spending like it's going out of fashion. I'm starting to cash up ready for the bank in the morning, which is the last banking day before Christmas. It's the busiest week of the year, of course, and there's bugger all electronic payments back then. Cash is king and we're minting the stuff. Three blokes walk in. Two of them stay in the shop and the other one walks into the back with a gun, Ross Aaron Robinson. That's where I am. He takes me for a raw prawn, but I stay calm because Angelo Junior is helping out in the store. Angelo is thirteen years old. Robinson is nineteen years old. His mates start yelling at my staff and customers out front, and it goes pear shaped. I can hear a scuffle and something getting bust up. Robinson gets a dead dingo's dick up him and botches it. Then he loses it completely and shoots me twice. The police arrive just before I die. End of story? Don't you believe it. The story never ended.

I was a protector for my family, and they never let me down. Mary kept it all going with my ghost by her side. Each of our boys, Angelo Junior, Daniel and Chris, made the same decision. Each one of them graduated high school one day and started working as Gamesmen the next. They've kept my dream going, and I reckon they've made a decent living together. More than that, they built an empire.

But emperors can be softies too. Every morning, one of our sons opens up our superstore in Penshurst, walks to the far corner and turns on an old TV set. Then he loads a game into a vintage Atari 2600. The controller's a bit crook, the TV colours are a bit saturated, and the picture flickers a bit, but it all works. Of course it's the Rank Arena that Mary and me got given for our wedding. And it stays on from the minute we open to the minute we close, seven days a week without fail. It hasn't broken down yet.

"Keep moving forward," I tell them. "Computer games are your games now."

Angelo Cusumano, 1982
with grateful acknowledgement to
Mary Cusumano, Lisa Paglia and David West

Chris, Daniel, Mary, Angelo Junior, 2022
with grateful acknowledgement to
Mary Cusumano, Lisa Paglia and David West

The Eighteenth Ghost

Danielle Bunten Berry 1949-1998

The Multiplayer Game, 1983

W hen I was a little boy called Dan, the only time my family spent together that wasn't totally dysfunctional was when we were playing games. That's the reason I always believed games were the most wonderful way anyone can socialize. I was the oldest of six in our family, growing up in Little Rock, Arkansas USA, and I guess we didn't have enough money for vacations and stuff, so our cheapest leisure option was always gaming. I was in the Scouts for a while and then I took little paid jobs when I was at school. One time I was working for a bit of money at the local pharmacy when the guy running it told my parents I was bright enough to apply for university. They couldn't afford it, so I funded myself through the University of Arkansas by running my own bike shop that I called The Highroller.

I started writing text-based adventure games for fun when business was slack, which was most of the time, and after I got my degree in industrial engineering I got more and more into programming. My first commercial title was called *Wheeler Dealers* which was an auction game for the Apple II. I sold it to a Canadian company called Speakeasy, but my introduction to the commercial gaming world was far from easy. My game needed a custom controller which put the cost up to a stupid level, thirty five dollars at a time when other games cost ten or fifteen, and my game sold less than fifty copies. That would have been in 1978. The following year a guy called Joe Billings founded a wargame software house called Strategic Simulations over in Mountain View, California, and I sold him my next three games. So I sort of became a full time games creator, and I branded my ideas as Ozark Softscape because I was a mountain boy.

Like all computer game development teams back then, Ozark was run by accident and not with any great plan, with an ideas guy like me and some techie friends, but usually without anyone who could run the business side of things effectively. In our case it was me, my brother Bill, Jim Rushing, and Alan Watson, and we operated out of my basement right there in Little Rock. And there at the other end of the food chain was the most famous guy in American gaming at the time, Trip Hawkins. He'd been at Apple since the very start in 1978, and in 1982 when he went and founded his own games company, he was already aware of my games for Strategic Simulations. He had this vision that gaming was going to be huge, and that game creators were not technicians but artists, which is why he called his company Electronic Arts. And that's why the packaging for my breakthrough game was sold in a big square format like a record album. Trip Hawkins modelled his titles on the music business, so I guess he thought of me as a rock star as much as a gamer.

Well, I guess it's time to talk about that breakthrough title of mine, but first it's important to understand that up to then video games were for single players, or for head-to-head gaming where each player took turns, or for match-type games like tennis. But ever since Atari launched their 400 and

800 systems in 1979 there had been absolutely no need for that sort of restriction because Atari provided four joystick ports that allowed simultaneous play. So in theory, a multi-player strategy game was not only possible, but practical. The joke was right there in the name of my game, I called it *M.U.L.E.* and that could stand for Multiple Use Labor Element or Mining Utility Lift Engine or Multi User Leading Entertainment, but in the real world a mule is a cross between a donkey and a horse, and it can be stubborn, mean and run off out of control. When Electronic Arts released it in their first batch of titles in 1983 the critics labelled it "ahead of its time", but a whole load of gamers ignored them and they got completely hooked on my gameplay.

I was always a sci-fi nut, and I lifted the setting for my game from a great book by Robert A. Heinlein called *Time Enough For Love*, where he questioned the whole morality of human civilisation. I didn't actually raise those questions in the game, but I did allow players to create their own futures. Players took the part of a mining prospector colonist on a distant planet I named Irata. Their mission was to build the planet's economy by gathering food, generating energy and sourcing precious minerals and ores, then manufacture stuff they could sell at a profit, just like in the Mabel Addis *Sumerian Game.* And like her, I included a swell randomization engine for disaster events like meteor strikes and sunspots, which helped level the playing field and make sure the game was nice and open. But my killer element was an auction system where players could make bids to buy and sell land and resources in real time at the start of each phase of the game.

I know the graphics were limited, all blocky and without a lot of detail, and I know the audio effects were really crude, but it was the real-time element that got the gamers coming back again and again. There was a proper sense of urgency when they played. As for the robot M.U.L.E.s, they actually looked like giant donkeys plodding around the planet, and I gave each of them different abilities for the players to manage. The little theme song was catchy too, I was very happy with that.

As it turned out, sales were a lot lower than I'd hoped for at less than 30,000 units, and that's because piracy was on the increase big time. Those were the days of games on floppy discs, and illegal copying was incredibly cheap and easy. I wanted to develop games for cartridge-based systems, but when Trip Hawkins refused to consider it I quit Electronic Arts. To tell the truth, we had one hell of a dispute. I had given him his biggest game of the year with my follow-up to *M.U.L.E* called *Seven Cities of Gold*, and I knew damn well that my work kept him out of the bankruptcy court. In fact, things didn't go too well for me then, and my team split up and moved on, and I dissolved Ozark Softscape.

Here in the afterlife, I'm not at all surprised to see that more has been written about my personal life than my gaming life, so let's get that over with. I was married three times, and I was father to a daughter and two sons. After my third divorce I had surgery for sex reassignment and transitioned from a man to a woman. Dan Bunten became Danielle Bunten Berry, take it or leave it. Sure, I sort of regretted it, and the gaming industry treated me like shit. I wrote an open letter to them saying that being my 'real self' could have included having a penis and more femininity in whatever forms made sense. But I didn't know that until it was too late and I had to make the best of the life I stumbled into. I just wish I would have tried more options before I jumped off the precipice. I'm sorry I lost so many of my former friends and colleagues because of my drinking and behaviour towards them, but that's how it was.

Changing sex in some big city like San Francisco would hardly raise an eyebrow, but the fact is I stayed in small-town conservative Little Rock to be close to my children, and most people disowned me, including my ex-wives and my mother. Did I mention that I stood six feet two inches tall, and the games industry had known me as their one and only good-old boy always up for some football, beer and dirty talk? I had to learn to walk, speak and dress as a woman, and as a woman I had to sing when I spoke and dance when I walked. Female speech is like a song, we have a lot more melody and different speech patterns. Walking is really a bit like dancing, slower and connected, with a lot of subtle movements. I enjoyed it at once. One thing I missed was not being able to aim when I peed, but that was a small sacrifice.

After I transitioned I kept out of the video game spotlight and kept to myself until I died of lung cancer age 49, just after the Computer Game Developers Association gave me their Lifetime Achievement Award. Thanks a bunch guys.

Gaming? Like I told them at the time, no one on their death bed ever said, I wish I had spent more time alone with my computer!

Dani Bunten Berry, 1995
with acknowledgement to The Women's Centre
University of Maryland Baltimore County

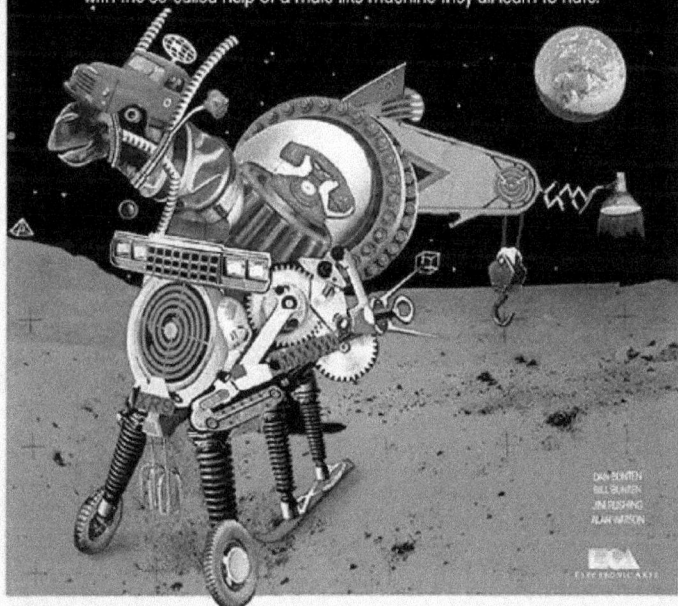

M.U.L.E. album–style game box for Atari 5200
Mel Croucher, private archive

The Nineteenth Ghost

Doris Self, 1925-2006

Pro Competitive Gaming, 1984

S ome ghosts live a long long time, but all they do is
repeat the same sequence time after time after time in a
sort of endless loop. And in my case, my afterlife is very
much like my real life, where I'm trapped hopping around a
pyramid swearing at a bunch of weird critters. Sure, I know
some ghosts manage to haunt a whole lot of different
machines, but in my case there's only one that I haunt. It's
called Q*bert, and because of it I became the most famous pro
gamer in the world at a time when I was 58 years old. And
that's not all. I was 81 years old and I was still practicing for
my next world record on Q*bert when I got killed in an auto
wreck. So put your seat belt on, buckle up good, and if you're
ready I'll take you for the ride through my life. Here we go.

When I was still in my teens, I got a job working for a
wonderful man called Eddie Rickenbacker, who was the most
famous and most decorated US flying ace of World War One.
In 1945, Eddie was boss of Eastern Air Lines and I was one of

his first-class airline stewardesses. It was me who founded the Silverliners association in 1954, which was the first organisation for lady crew members. The twin-prop Douglas DC3 I used to fly is still hanging high up there from the ceiling at the National Air and Space Museum in Washington DC.

After I retired from flying I got the Silverliners to organise charity events at airports all over the world doing what we called our Flights To The North Pole, where we'd take really sick kids to meet Santa Claus each Christmas. I don't know who loved that more, the kids or me. I still flew every chance I got, and then I got involved with cars and horses too. I went fox hunting with three different sets, you know, not the rip-em-apart kind of fox hunting, ours was the hounds chasing the scent with the horses chasing the hounds type. While my husband Paul and our son Randy were still alive, Christmas was our most special family time, in fact I always used to have seven Christmas trees.

There was a ten foot living tree, for the ornaments I collected on my world travels, like my Amazonian shrunken head. There was a big old white tree for gold and glitter stuff that I made myself from costume jewelry and tic-tac boxes. And I had a fantasy tree with little dragons and witches and stuff, I think that was my favorite. Randy's favorite was the bear tree that was full of every bear you can imagine from ice-skaters to dancing bears in tuxedos. The sci-fi tree was exactly as you'd imagine, with all the stuff from Star Trek and the Star Wars movies. I kept our table-top tree for miniature presents all wrapped up, and hundreds of twinkly lights. And of course there was the talking tree that sat on another table draped in a cloth to hide the loudspeaker. Last but not least was the pool tree, and that one floated about on an inflatable tube, moving around thanks to the pool pump and driving the neighbours crazy. I would invite them in to play poker to defuse things. I was a pretty good gambler and I held some swell poker nights, and I was usually a winner at the craps tables too. But it was arcade gaming that really got me. I was a great gamer.

I was introduced to the arcades by my daughter Kerri soon after the first arcade machines came along in the late 70s. I think I played my first arcade screen in a Chuck E Cheese diner. I had just become a widow and although Q*Bert could never replace my husband I guess he was the next best thing. I used to haunt the arcades, especially the 24 hour one about ten minutes from where I lived, where you might find me racking 'em up in the early hours and into the morning. In fact they couldn't keep me out. And I'll tell you something with no false modesty, I was better than all the rest. I could beat the pants off anyone who reckoned they could best my hi-scores. I'd usually wait until eleven at night and go over there and start gaming. There were a lot of young people in there and I had so much fun with the older teens. Sometimes I wouldn't get home until seven in the morning. But that's the way I am. When I really get into something I go all the way to the end of the line.

I guess the reason I got to be famous was not just because I was a woman, or even because I was an older woman, but it was that I became a pro gamer at a time when gamers were just unpaid enthusiasts. I know that nowadays gamers can earn really big money and the audiences are huge, but it all had to start somewhere so it might as well have started with me. Yes I got paid some prize money, and I got to be world champion too. They even made a film about me called *A Fistful of Quarters*, or *The King of Kong* all about my mission to win back my title as the world's oldest gaming champion. Anyways, I first won my title in 1984 when I got into the Guinness World Records playing my all-time favourite game, *Q*Bert*. So now it's time for me tell you all about the game.

*Q*Bert* is what I call an all-action game. It was a coin-slot made by the Gottlieb company, who had been making pinball machines for a generation before the video arcades came along, and it cost a quarter to play each time. The cabinet was a lot bigger than I was, and it was painted with the characters from the game. By the time it was retired from service, it had become Gottlieb's most popular game by a very long way.

Q*Bert has a really basic two-dimensional layout, but it looks sort of 3D on the screen because the cubes that make up the pyramid play area are shaded. The gameplay idea is really simple too, all you do is move a 4-way joystick to control your Q*Bert cartoon character to hop on top of a cube and make it change color, that's how you increase your score. There are obstacles and critters that get in your way, and Q*Bert will swear when he gets blocked. Well, not real cussing, it's more like a baby swearing noise with a speech balloon for grawlix symbols.

You always start at the top of the pyramid, which is made up of 28 cubes and is 7 cubes tall, and you move diagonally. Once you change the color on all the cubes you go on to the next level. At the easiest level it's enough just to jump on every cube once, but as the levels get harder you have to jump on twice, or maybe they revert to the original color if you hit them, or colors change for all sorts of other reasons. And if you jump off the pyramid, well, your Q*Bert dies and it's game over. You also die if a critter gets you.

My favourite enemy critter was Coily, who starts out as a purple egg then hatches into a snake and chases you. There's Wrongway and Ugg who move up the pyramid and kill you if they get in your way, and Slick and Sam who move down the pyramid who don't kill you but they change the color back and mess up your gameplay. What else now? Oh yeah, there's bad bouncing red balls that take a life, and good bouncing green balls that freeze the other critters for a while, and colored floaty discs that take you to the top of the pyramid if you jump on one.

As for the scores, it's 15 or 20 every time a cube changes color, killing Coily with a flying disc gets you 500, bonus discs earn 50 or 100, there's another 100 for catching a green ball or getting Sam or Slick, and there are bonus points for completing each pyramid, 1,000 up to 5,000. The machine operators have a setting where they can control extra lives for hitting a preset score, but of course the player has no control over that. OK folks, wait for it, at the Twin Galaxies Video Game Masters Tournament on July first 1984, I scored the world record Q*Bert result of 1,112,300 points and I was awarded World's Oldest Video Game Champion too. What can I say! Well, I can say nobody remains the champ forever, and one day the inevitable happened and my record got broken. But I battled to win back my crown until the day I became a ghost.

As late as 2005 I was playing professionally for the championship world record, that was in London at the Classic Gaming Expo. And two days later I was in Paris as a member of the US National Video Game Team. The following year in Florida I got challenged by Kelly Tharp in front of a huge audience for what they called the 'King versus Queen Q*Bert Smackdown', and it was down there in the Everglades near my home in Plantation that I died in the automobile wreck on my way to a practice session for my next world record attempt. So don't you ever accuse me of being a quitter. I played at every major casino in the world while I was alive and I'll be waiting for you at that great crap table in the sky. Don't forget though, I'll be playing to win.

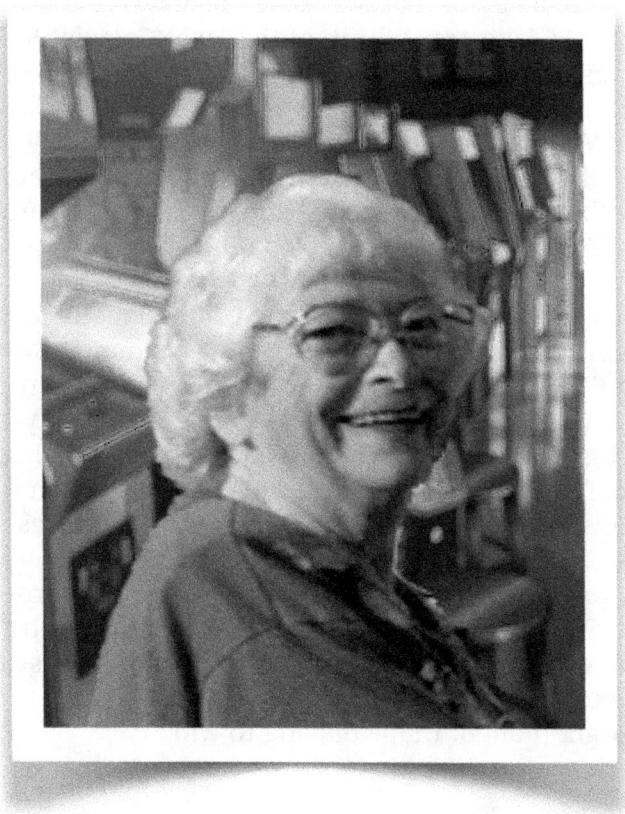

Doris Self, aged 74
with grateful thanks to Kerri Self & ACAM non-profit organisation

Q*Bert screen
Mel Croucher, private archive

The Twentieth Ghost

Karel Twisten Asenbrener 2003-2023

The Ghost In The Machine, 2023

I've never heard of the other ghosts in this book. Why would I? Gaming was always part of my life, so everything already happened to make gaming the way it was before I was born. It's like me saying to you, name the ghosts in the motor car. Like who invented the electric motor, or the rubber tyre, or the headlamp, or the nav system? You don't know, and it's the same for me with gaming. I mean the ghosts who came before me are history. They have no meaning for me, you know.

Ghosts only stay alive as long as people remember the dead person, which means I'm alive in the memories of my friends and family, and also for huge numbers of gamers. 325 million esport viewers. The top players earn guap, like over five million dollars a year. And I nearly got to the top.

My name is Karel, my friends called me Kaja, my fans called me Twisten. Twisten means to capture. It means to win, to argue. It can also mean to take someone's virginity. I will be remembered for two things, for sure, for being a cult gamer and for being mentally ill. It was Twisten who was the hero. It was Kaja who committed suicide. I was nineteen years old when I died.

I was born in Prague, that's the Czech capitol, in 2003. I knew nothing of my country's history. I mean, personally. Why would I? For me my country has always been in the European Union, which is great for young people. And for me my city has always been a great place for gamers to grow up. Like I loved to compete. I loved to win. I loved the applause. I was a great snowboarder. I played football for ČAFC Prague, but they were in the fifth division, you know what I mean, so they just weren't big enough for me. I was a winner. I was a leader. I was cool looking. I was funny. I was popular. I was scared of the *Miminka*.

Miminka means babies in English. When I was around six years old, ten giant *Miminka* appeared one morning crawling up the Prague TV tower. Like they really were giants, I mean they were metres long. All shiny and black. And they had barcodes instead of faces. They were monsters. And like they were out to get me.

I got into gaming early. I played my older brothers when they let me. Their favourite was *Fifa Soccer 10*, which was great, but my favourite was *Counter-Strike : Global Offensive*. I was really good at it. We played it on their old Xbox 360 and my Playstation 3, even before I was ten years old. *CS:GO* was a first-person shooter, but what I loved was the multiplayer side. It was free to play, but I had to pay for all the extra stuff. Like to earn points that I could spend, I had to win. And I had to win big time. No cap.

I could play Terrorist or Counter-Terrorist. I could plant a bomb or defuse it. I could capture hostages or free them. But for me the exciting part was matchmaking. We did matchmaking on special servers, where I was allowed to add custom maps and my own play modes. It was the start of the whole esports ride for me.

I worked my way up the gamer food chain. I got hooked early. All my socials were with gamers. Facebook, YouTube,

Insta, Twitter, you know. When I wasn't on socials I was gaming. I started out with the eSuba team. They won the Samsung Europeans and then like they fell to pieces, I mean really. The team captain Herdyn took them to the top of the Czech season. I was in my teens by then. Next thing I joined the Entropiq crew. They were pros with attitude and cool merch, but though I was big, I was only big in my own country, and like I say, that wasn't big enough. I loved my fans, but I wanted more. Yeah.

By then I got a taste for tournaments. Not as a watcher, like as a player. I joined the BIG Clan, from Berlin. World class. Top leagues. Pro players. Iykyk. I turned 16.

In 2020 Riot Games released *Valorant*, inspired by my personal best game *Counter-Strike*. It had like the same buy menu and the same spray patterns. I mean it even had the same shooter handicaps when you move. It was the first person tactical hero shooter. *Valorant* was my life. I became famous. I became Twisten. I moved to the French outfit Team Vitality, but we were all nationalities. The fans said I was important, but I was not important. The game was important and the team was important, you know. But for me, like when I was onstage, the fans were most important.

When I died, my mother, Ivana, she said like, "Karel was a clown, he loved tournaments that took place right on the stage, he loved his fans and he loved the audience. During the breaks he used gestures that made him memorable among the gaming community. First, he would send his opponents a heart, which he represented with his fingers, then he used the Korean symbol for love, which is a kind of snapping of the fingers, and his third typical gesture was cat ears, which he made with his hands."

I guess that's a bit weird, but I want to tell you why *Valorant* is so special. For me it made team esports a lot more accessible to new players, and to tactical shooters, and to professionals. And it was designed to bring in the biggest competitive scene ever. Like arena audiences. I mean big audiences. Huge audiences. And *Valorant* was designed for really low hardware standards, you know. A max ping of 35 millisecs for at least seven out of ten players. 128-tick servers in every major city on the planet, with dedicated connections. Do you get what I'm saying?

We played in teams of five. Five attackers and five defenders. The competitive matches had win-based ranking. I got a new rank after every five games. I started with a classic pistol and worked my way up to automatics with unique shooting patterns, you know. Then instead of sudden death rounds, I started to play win-by-twos, playing alternate attack and defence to get a two-match lead. Then I went in for Deathmatch and Escalation modes. And Replication, where I could vote on which agent I wanted to become. After a kill, I got like a green health pack with new armour and max ammo, and got respawned anywhere on the map.

I could get girlfriends, I mean in real life, but that didn't always work out so well, you know. And I made a lot of money gaming esports. All us top players in the world made a lot of money. I'm not going to big myself up, but I want you to know that I gave a lot of my money to kid's charities. Like the Turkish earthquake in 2023. That was four months before I died.

Look, I have to tell you that it isn't just girlfriend mess or earthquake disaster that made me depressed. COVID was terrible, you know, specially for my generation. 2020, just when I hit it big. My country had the worst increase for anxiety, for depression because of COVID. Over fifteen per cent of people my age.

I spoke out about my depression, I wasn't afraid to do that, and I got sent to see specialists, like I say, I got treatment. But. When I killed myself in 2023, suicide caused more deaths in my age group in the Czech Republic than any other reason. Yeah. I killed myself. I could kill all my enemies in *Valorant*, but I couldn't kill my own demons. Ha! I dealt with it somehow for more than two years. Longer. I don't know if people saw how bad I was at the LOCK/IN tournament my last Christmas, you know, in Brazil. But, like I did bad things to myself. You know, self-harm.

I felt like killing myself then, when I self-harmed, but my dad saved me. I spent time in the mental health hospital for bad cases. For people with serious problems like I had. When I got out I told my teammates and my fans I was doing great. Like mentally and physically. And I thanked them, and promised them 2023 would be our best freaking year ever. I broke my promise. There was no glow up.

My last tweet was viewed by four million fans. It was just "Good night." Yeah, I know. I should have tweeted my favourite quote from *Demon Slayer* Rengoku. But I didn't.

"If you are feeling disheartened, that you are somehow not enough, set your heart ablaze. Dry your eyes and look ahead. You may feel like digging your heels in, but the flow of time waits for no one. It won't patiently stand by as you grieve. Don't feel bad that I'm going to die."

Karel Ašenbrener, selfie, 2023
with acknowledgement and thanks to the Ašenbrener family,
in support of Mental Health Europe, co-funded by the European Union

Esports arena crowd, 2025
photo with kind permission of Stockcake, ref. 557420_1144383
for copyright-free usage

AUTHOR'S POSTSCRIPT

From the first moment I programmed a computer back in 1969, I knew that its true purpose was to entertain people. I remember using punch cards to tame a great beast of a machine filled with glowing valves and spaghetti wiring, and turn it into a device for the sort of dopey gaming that could amuse a simple soul like me. The machine belonged to the Ministry of Defence and I belonged to the Campaign for Nuclear Disarmament, but we coexisted for the six months it took me to invent a primitive multi-media contraption and sync coloured lights in response to pop music until the gamer fell asleep in abject boredom.

Gaming should be an incredibly positive experience and it should be joyous. But it's a sad fact that in the world of gaming, as exemplified by our final Ghost in the Machine, suicide now accounts for a quarter of all deaths in the 15 to 24 age group. According to the National Statistical Office, one in three school-leavers experiences moderate to severe anxiety, and four in ten suffer from depression.

As well as anxiety and depression, habitual gamers have a higher incidence of other negative factors on their mental health. For example, the violence that is inherent in many games can normalise aggression for players. What starts as fun and escapism may lead to avoidance of real-life emotional challenges and a dependence on fantasies. The isolation involved in excessive gaming often leads to ignoring real-life friendships and social connections, which are major factors in depression. Social anxiety is rife among gamers, usually triggered by false expectations, trolling, fakes and vindictive attacks on social media. And in addition to all that, disrupted sleep patterns and the lack of sleep caused by excessive gaming is a major factor in the worsening of any pre-existing mental health condition.

As the founder of the first video-games company in the UK, I suppose I must share some of the responsibility for starting it all off. To be honest, I didn't have a clue what the implications could be, and when I eventually recognised the problems and pitfalls I knew I should have shouted louder than I did. I tried my best to call out the cynics and exploiters, but I guess I just didn't try hard enough. I took the easy way out and just turned my back for several decades. Because I could.

This book is a celebration of gaming, and a celebration of the key figures who made it all happen, but it is not a glorification. The fact that you read these words in printed form tells me that in all probability you are of an age and mentality to avoid the pitfalls of excessive gaming. But maybe you know someone who is at risk, a neighbour, a colleague, a family member. And if you do, then I encourage you to do something about it. The telltale signs are self evident, but I'll list them anyway.

- Showing withdrawal symptoms when not gaming, such as irritability or gloom or anxiety.
- Consistently using video games as a form of escapism.
- Lying to loved ones about how much time is spent gaming.
- Prioritising gaming over relationships and other social activities.
- A need to spend more and more time gaming to feel the original pleasure.
- Performing poorly at school or at work because of excessive gaming.
- Reducing time spent on personal hygiene and grooming.
- Trying to relieve negative emotions like hopelessness or guilt by gaming.

- The inability to reduce gameplay or to quit games despite being aware of these factors.

The Ašenbrener family have set up a foundation in the Czech Republic to help young people who find themselves in a similar situation to Twisten. His mother Ivana says this, on behalf of her husband and their two surviving sons:
"Karel's suicide is still a very painful thing for the whole family. Yet we decided, and for the sake of our son, to turn the pain into something meaningful. Our foundation aims to help other young people with mental health problems. I'm sure my son would agree and support it."
https://www.twistenfoundation.cz/en

There is similar help available in your area, either locally or nationally. A simple search on a phrase like "excessive gaming" will lead you in the right direction. If you love your gaming, then love gamers too. Thank you for reading this.

Mel Croucher, 2025

THE GAMERS HALL OF FAME

thank you for helping to make this project happen

Llaura McGee

Andrew Fisher

Craig Howard

Paul

Anna-Maria Kwasny

Joe Wade

Neil Kenny

Rob Gregorczyk

Grant Forrest

THE GAMERS HALL OF FAME

thank you for helping to make this project happen

Andrew Kenny

Ivan Oranciuc

Richard Hallas

Robert Mendez

Tango Bunny

John Arrasjid

Winnie Minkey

Thibault Jaillon

Brian Rizo

THE GAMERS HALL OF FAME
thank you for helping to make this project happen

Steve Randall

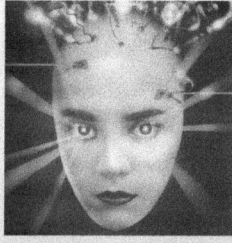

Shane Mengaziol

Gordon
Eyton-Williams

Liv Ex Machina

Paul Monaghan

The Das Family

Rene Genest

Mary Eliza

Matt Birch

THE GAMERS HALL OF FAME

thank you for helping to make this project happen

Jon Douglas

Rosalie Jackson

Matthias Rich

Derek Chandler

Eric *Gronkh* Range

Nicola Russo

Tony Lucignano Jr.

THE GAMERS HALL OF FAME
thank you for being there

Rick Foyle

Jas Austin

Robin Evans

Tom Christie

Julie Christie

Jaro Švelch

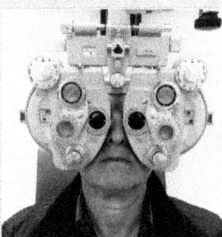

Marek Zawadzki

Colin Jones

Frank Z

THE GAMERS ROLL OF HONOUR
thank you for helping to make this project happen

Andrew Fisher
Andrew Kenny
Anna-Maria Kwasny
Anthony Lucignano
Ash
Bill Sheakoski
Carl Harris
Chris Sewell
Christopher Wright
Craig Howard
the Das Family
Dave Steele
David Isherwood
Derek Chandler
Erik 'Gronkh' Range
Frank Z
Fredrik Claesson
Gordon Eyton-Williams
Grant Forrest
Ivan Oranciuc
Jaro Švelch
Jas Austin
Javier M Moreno

THE GAMERS ROLL OF HONOUR
thank you for helping to make this project happen

Jens Radeke
Jesse Glenn
Joe Wade
John Arrasjid
Jon Douglas
Julie Christie
Jurre Zwierstra
Liv Ex Machina
Llaura Mcgee
Marc Lafontaine
Marek Zawadzki
Mary Eliza
Matt Birch
Matthias Rich
Neil Kenny
Nicola Russo
Paul Desmond
Paul Monaghan
PR Taylor
Rene Genest
Richard Hallas
Rick Foyle
Rob Gregorczyk

THE GAMERS ROLL OF HONOUR
thank you for helping to make this project happen

Robert Mendez
Robin Evans
Rosalie Jackson
Sean Smith
Shane Mengaziol
Steve Barrett
Steve Randall
Steven Gailey
Tango Bunny
Thibault Jaillon
Tom Christie
Tony Lucignano Jr.
Winnie Minkey

other publications
by MEL CROUCHER

Pimania the Final Solution (with Robin Evans)
1982, Automata

101 Uses of a Dead Cruise Missile (with Robin Evans), 1983, Scorpio
Ltd / PCND

The Back Pages (with Robin Evans)
1983-1985, Sunshine Publications, weekly

Tamara Knight
1986, Newsfield Publications, monthly

Mercy Dash (with Robin Evans)
1986-1988, Dennis Publishing, monthly

Rebel of World Zero (with Robin Evans)
1987-1988, EMAP Publications, monthly

Without Prejudice
1987-1989, Stranger Than Fiction, monthly

Frozen Stiffs (with Robin Evans)
1987-1989, Stanger Than Fiction, monthly

Namesakes (with Jon Pertwee)
1988, Sphere Books, ISBN 780747400233

European Computer Trade Yearbook (Editor)
1988-1995, ECTA, annually

Zygote, Last Words
1988-2020, Dennis Publishing, monthly

AMOS Professional
1989, Europress, ISBN 0951953214

Sam Coupé
1989, Miles Gordon Technology, ISBN 9781785388613

Easy AMOS
1992, Europress, ISBN 781872084527

e-media
2000, Institute of Practitioners in Advertising,
ISBN 1841160555

Deus Ex Machina
2014, Acorn Books, 9781783336937

From Bedrooms to Billions (as himself)
2014, Gracious Films, ISBN 700461458784

Devil's Acre
2015, Acorn Books, ISBN 978-1837910731

Great Moments In Computing (with Robin Evans)
2017, Acorn Books, ISBN 9781785387579

Pibolar Disorder (with Robin Evans)
2017, Acorn Books, ISBN 9781785388330

Short Pants (with Robin Evans)
2017, Acorn Books, ISBN 9781785388309

Last Orders
2017, AG Books ISBN 1785386417

Memoirs of a Spectrum Addict (as himself)
2017-2020, RAM Films

Mel Croucher the Audiobook
2017, Oak Tree Press/Andrews UK, ASIN B074VHGZMD

Great Moments in Computing, the Complete Edition
2022, Acorn Books, ISBN 9781789829242

Mundaneum
2024, Extremis Publishing, ISBN 9781739484569

Additional details of Mel Croucher's work are available on the
Wikipedia page: https://en.wikipedia.org/wiki/Mel_Croucher

Also Available from Extremis Publishing

MUNDANEUM

The Shocking True Story of the Man
who Invented the Internet and the Man
who Destroyed It

By Mel Croucher

This is the true story of two men who meet only once. One is a pacifist, the other is a Nazi. Both men are visionaries, but their visions for the future of the world cannot be more different.

One man's vision is to harness data for peace, and a century ago he builds a world-wide-web to deliver exactly that. The other man's vision is to harness information to control the masses, and in 1944 he achieves that too.

This is the shocking truth about the man who invented the Internet and the man who destroyed it.

Also Available from Extremis Publishing

DIGITAL PIONEER SPIRIT

The Freewheeling Creative Innovation
of Mel Croucher on the Home
Microcomputer

By Thomas A. Christie

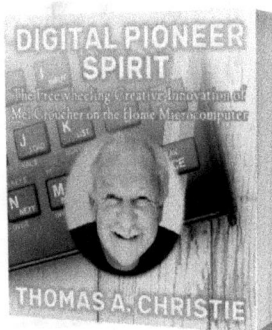

Get ready to step into the revolutionary world of Mel Croucher – a genuine maverick who redefined the digital age. In *Digital Pioneer Spirit*, Thomas A. Christie unravels the extraordinary career of the man who blazed a trail as Britain's first multimedia personality.

Mel Croucher was a virtuoso talent even in an age of innovators. From his ground-breaking computer games like *PiMania*, *iD*, and *Deus Ex Machina* – a cult classic that fused gaming, art, and music – to his razor-sharp journalism and visionary writing, Croucher's work shattered boundaries and challenged conventions. A counter-cultural genius with a boundlessly whimsical sense of humour, he stood as an iconoclast in the earliest days of the home computer industry, harnessing emerging technology to inspire, provoke, and entertain.

With meticulous research, Christie paints a compelling portrait of a creative rebel whose influence still ripples through today's digital culture. Whether you're a tech enthusiast, a gaming historian, or an admirer of unconventional minds, *Digital Pioneer Spirit* is an unmissable exploration of the man who turned bits and bytes into a bold new art form.

Discover the amazing true story of Mel Croucher – a digital pioneer, a cultural provocateur, and a true original.

For details of new and forthcoming books from Extremis Publishing, including our monthly podcasts, please visit our official website at:

www.extremispublishing.com

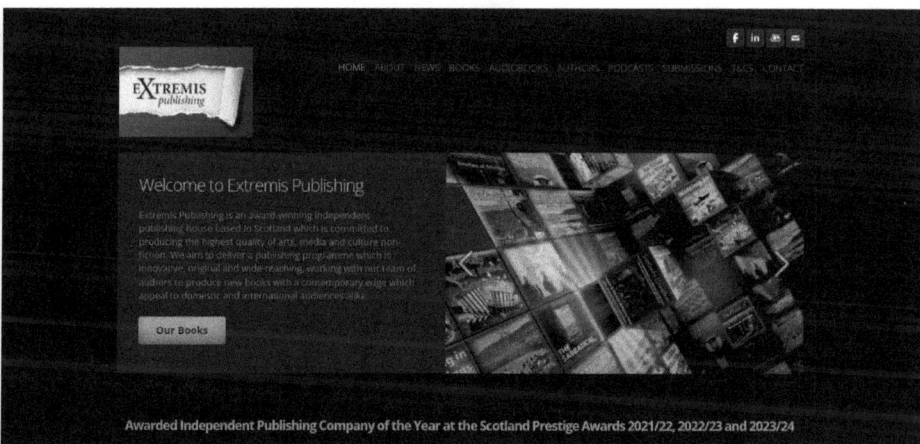

Awarded Independent Publishing Company of the Year at the Scotland Prestige Awards 2021/22, 2022/23 and 2023/24

or follow us on social media at:

www.facebook.com/extremispublishing

www.linkedin.com/company/extremis-publishing-ltd-/